Early praise for *Fixing Your Sc*

Ken Schwaber, the co-creator of Scrum, often says that Scrum takes a moment to understand and a lifetime to master. Scrum isn't hard to understand, but applying it is difficult because the environments in which Scrum plays are complex. People, organizations, business problems, suppliers, predefined processes, and behavioral norms all seem to work against this simple framework. In this book, Todd and Ryan provide practical remedies to these problems. They focus on ways that you can make your use of Scrum better, not because Scrum is important, but because—when applied well—Scrum can help you change the world. Scrum on!

➤ **Dave West**
CEO, Scrum.org

This book is a friendly and conversational partner for today's Scrum Master. It provides real-world solutions to real-world problems that many teams face in pursuit of being truly self-organized and cross-functional. Ryan and Todd have identified some of the most common anti-patterns that result in bad experiences and less-than-optimal outcomes with Scrum–and encourage teams to face them with practical tools and humor.

➤ **Melissa Boggs**
Chief ScrumMaster, Scrum Alliance

Scrum: So few instructions, yet so many misunderstandings. Ryan and Todd offer you a multitude of ways to get your Scrum back on track. Not for the sake of Scrum or "theory," but for the sake of addressing real-world problems. Use their combined experiences and expertise to remove long-lived obfuscation and fix your Scrum.

➤ **Gunther Verheyen**
Independent Scrum Caretaker

If everyone would follow Ryan and Todd's vision of what a Scrum master should be, then Scrum (with Kanban, of course) would be near perfect!

➤ **Daniel Vacanti**
CEO, Actionable Agile

As an Agile coach, I constantly encounter organizations that are doing Scrum poorly and missing out on the great results and impact that Scrum can have. Ryan and Todd's book has become my go-to initial action for these organizations —I hand them the book and tell them to read it and apply its simple yet powerful advice. It does a masterful job of helping teams fix their Scrum. Now I just hope it doesn't impact my coaching practice too much!

➤ **Bob Galen**
   Author and Agile Coach, Vaco

This book is an essential read for any Scrum team that wants to deliver value frequently and enjoy doing it. It illuminates the most common Scrum anti-patterns, explains their underlying causes, and offers practical ways to overcome them. You'll appreciate both the directness and the humility in the authors' positive approach to fixing your Scrum.

➤ **Stephanie Ockerman**
   Professional Scrum Trainer and Author, Agile Socks, LLC

If people read this book before implementing with Scrum, they wouldn't need to do much fixing! Ryan and Todd did an excellent job creating a well-structured compendium that you can read in order and/or use as a powerful reference. In particular, the Coach's Corner section in each chapter is full of great, practical advice for every practicing Scrum master.

➤ **Ralph Jocham**
   Founder of Effective Agile and author of *The Professional Product Owner*

This book is going to put a lot of consultants out of business. It has the answers to some of the really tough questions and stumbling points for those using Scrum. Concise, clear, and to the point, this book is a must-have for Agile practitioners.

➤ **Dr. Charles Suscheck**
   CEO and Primary Trainer, Juniper Hill Associates

Ryan's and Todd's book is filled with practical solutions you can use to fix your Scrum. Every day, Scrum masters come to me asking for practical ideas they can quickly put into practice, and that's exactly the kind of advice that Ryan and Todd have put together for this actionable, takeaway-oriented book. It's a must-read for all Scrum masters who want to continuously improve their practice. Read it and then put it into practice!

➤ **Vasco Duarte**
   Host, Scrum Master Toolbox Podcast

Refreshing, practical, and down to earth. *Fixing Your Scrum* tackles day-to-day scenarios we've all seen as Scrum practitioners. Ryan and Todd avoid the dogma and instead share concrete solutions they've experimented with in the trenches, and explain what makes these solutions work in a Scrum context. This book deserves a prominent space on your Scrum/Agile bookshelf.

➤ **Yuval Yeret**
  CTO, AgileSparks

Todd and Ryan have assembled an invaluable reference for common Scrum missteps. If your organization and teams haven't been realizing all of the benefits that Scrum and agility offer, this book offers lots of empathetic and practical guidance for improvement.

➤ **Faye Thompson**
  Chair, Central Ohio Agile Association

Wow—I've found my new go-to guide for Scrum team success! Ryan and Todd offer practical suggestions and guidance to fix almost every Scrum issue I've encountered over my 12 years as an Agile coach and Scrum master. They also provide exercises and self-reflective questions to help me improve my skills. This book will be invaluable to me and my future teams.

➤ **Jill Graves**
  Agile Coach/Scrum Master, Simply Scrum

This book is an essential companion for both seasoned Scrum practitioners and those taking their first steps. Ryan and Todd balance expert Scrum guidance with pragmatic advice for all. A must-have handbook for anyone who's serious about getting the best results possible with Scrum.

➤ **Zach Bonaker**
  Agile Coach, San Diego, CA

Fixing Your Scrum is a concise, direct coaching accelerator for Scrum teams seeking remedies to their problems. Page after page, it's full of thoughtful stories and wisdom-packed insights. This book is a must-read for all Scrum teams and managers!

➤ **Nabila Safdar**
  Scrum Master, Do it Best Corp.

In agile circles, we've talked for some time about the negative effects of modifying the Scrum framework, but no one has recorded those effects in writing—until now. Ryan and Todd brilliantly explain the various Scrum modifications they've experienced, identify the impacts of those modifications, and give helpful tips on how to effectively apply the framework to get the outcomes you want. This book is a must-read for all Scrum practitioners and managers of Scrum teams.

➤ **Joe Astolfi**
   Director of Agile, Columbus, OH

I would have loved to have had Ryan and Todd's book a few years ago. Scrum seems so easy to understand, but it's so difficult to master. Reading this book will save you from pitfalls and help you avoid painful moments.

➤ **Olivier Ledru**
   Professional Scrum Trainer with Scrum.org, Paris, France

This is the book I wish I had when I started doing Scrum. *Fixing Your Scrum* will help you understand the "why" behind Scrum, empower you to debug the systemic dysfunctions that impede organizational agility, and show you what not to do (so you can avoid shooting yourself in the foot). Read it. Apply it. Give it to others.

➤ **Ram Srinivasan**
   CST, CTC (Scrum Alliance), and PST (Scrum.org), InnovAgility.com

Ryan and Todd know how to create team dynamics that are powerful and inspirational. They offer advice that's very much worth your time to investigate and invest in.

➤ **Ty Crockett**
   Director, Improving

Fixing your Scrum identifies numerous anti-patterns that I've seen in my long career of helping organizations transform and change and become more agile. I've found that identifying the anti-patterns that are present in an organization helps get them back on track quickly. I wish I'd had this playbook to give to clients before working with them and to leave with them after. You'll see your organization and yourself in a lot of the examples in this book. Use its advice to ensure that you're inspecting and adapting your practices to make them better.

➤ **Dave Dame**
   Vice President of Global Agile, Scotiabank

Fixing your Scrum is about the future of Scrum teams around the world. It's a wonderful book about business value, empowerment, and quality, and it not only shows how these puzzle pieces fit together but also explains why. To all the Scrum team members out there who know that something's not right, this book can help you fix your Scrum now!

➤ **Joe Krebs**
Founder, Incrementor

Todd and Ryan hit a grand slam with this book. It's extremely thorough and easy to follow. I like that I can turn to a section of interest and get the information I'm seeking. It will be a must-read for everyone at Itero Group. I can't wait to pass out hard copies to our employees during orientations.

➤ **Jim Bailoni**
COO, Itero Group

Ryan and Todd have curated a thoughtful collection of the most common issues faced by Scrum practitioners with a wealth of solutions based on their experiences, which they share in colorful detail. I'll recommend this book to my students and clients as an excellent reference in the team room when Scrum gets hard.

➤ **Jason Tanner**
CEO and Co-founder, applied frameworks

In this book, Ryan and Todd share their experiences to help break down some of the most common challenges Scrum teams face. This is an immensely practical book I wish I'd had when I started using Scrum, and it's the book I still need for my work today.

➤ **Patricia Kong**
Product Owner, Enterprise Solutions, Scrum.org

Fixing Your Scrum

Practical Solutions to Common Scrum Problems

Ryan Ripley
Todd Miller

The Pragmatic Bookshelf

Raleigh, North Carolina

Many of the designations used by manufacturers and sellers to distinguish their products are claimed as trademarks. Where those designations appear in this book, and The Pragmatic Programmers, LLC was aware of a trademark claim, the designations have been printed in initial capital letters or in all capitals. The Pragmatic Starter Kit, The Pragmatic Programmer, Pragmatic Programming, Pragmatic Bookshelf, PragProg and the linking *g* device are trademarks of The Pragmatic Programmers, LLC.

Every precaution was taken in the preparation of this book. However, the publisher assumes no responsibility for errors or omissions, or for damages that may result from the use of information (including program listings) contained herein.

Our Pragmatic books, screencasts, and audio books can help you and your team create better software and have more fun. Visit us at *https://pragprog.com*.

The team that produced this book includes:

Publisher: Andy Hunt
VP of Operations: Janet Furlow
Executive Editor: Dave Rankin
Development Editor: Dawn Schanafelt
Copy Editor: Sean Dennis
Indexing: Potomac Indexing, LLC
Layout: Gilson Graphics

For sales, volume licensing, and support, please contact *support@pragprog.com*.

For international rights, please contact *rights@pragprog.com*.

ISBN-13: 978-1-68050-697-6
Book version: P1.0—January 2020

To my wife, Kristin. You make it all worth it.

—Ryan

To Jess, who makes the impossible possible for me.

—Todd

Contents

Foreword

Over my decades-long career, I've had the privilege of acting in all three of the Scrum roles: developer, Scrum master, and product owner. And I have a confession: I didn't always perform those roles well.

For example, I was once on a Scrum team that was horrible at breaking down work into something that could be completed in a sprint. It took months before we produced anything of value, which was incredibly demoralizing for the Scrum team and caused our stakeholders to disengage.

Then there was the time I was both the product owner and the Scrum master for the same Scrum team. I embraced being a Scrum master and invested the time required to be good at it——but that meant I didn't have time to be a good product owner. The result was a development team that excelled at turning out features that none of our customers wanted.

And even once I had become a decent Scrum master, I used to lean a little too much toward the servant part of being a servant leader. When I saw someone struggling with their role on a Scrum team, I would step in to help instead of letting them find their own way. That made it hard for people to learn how to self-organize.

As I look back on my career, I know I've learned from these missteps. But it would have saved me a lot of time, energy, and frustration if I'd had someone with more Scrum experience to guide me and help me avoid making these mistakes in the first place. While I wasn't lucky enough to have such a mentor, you are: the authors of this book.

In the following pages, Ryan and Todd share a ton of hard-earned lessons that they've learned during their careers. In their easy-to-absorb collection of examples, they offer advice for avoiding similar mistakes and for minimizing any damage from unfortunate choices you and/or your team might have already made.

Today, I'm an employee at Scrum.org, where my full-time job is to help professionals educate others about Scrum. But even though I'm a recognized expert in my field, I'm constantly learning new approaches and finding opportunities to improve my Scrum practice.

This book is full of practical suggestions that you can easily try for yourself. As you read this book and implement its advice, keep in mind that Scrum can be reduced to a small set of ideas:

Try something new.

See how it goes.

Repeat.

So if, like me, you need help with breaking down your work, or you're not sure who to select as your Scrum master, or you want to avoid being the Superhero Scrum Master, then this book is for you. You may even find a solution to a problem you didn't realize existed. I know that by the time I finished this book, I had several new ideas that I was eager to try.

Remember, your next sprint can always be better.

Ta.

Steve Porter

Team Member, Scrum.org

Acknowledgements

We both owe a huge debt of gratitude to Ken Schwaber and the Scrum.org staff. Because of Ken's vision and the Scrum.org team, we both have joyful careers that give us the opportunity to help people and organizations all over the world use Scrum to make the world a better place. Thank you Ken and the Scrum.org team.

We want to thank our tech reviewers for their invaluable help: Jesse Houwing, Jeff Langr, Amitai Schleier, Lucas Smith, Wilbert Seele, and Rich Visotcky. We'd also especially like to thank our editor, Dawn Schanafelt, for her help and support during the creation of this book. She made both of us sound far smarter and more articulate than we deserve.

Working with Pragmatic Bookshelf has been a great experience. We are truly grateful for the opportunity to collaborate on this project with Andy, Dave, and their amazingly talented team. Without them this book would not have been possible.

—Ryan and Todd

Preface

We're passionate about Scrum. In fact, we've both dedicated our lives to improving the profession of software delivery through training, coaching, and mentoring Scrum teams. In the pages that follow, you'll find strong opinions, new ideas, and a solid grounding in good Scrum practices. *Some of the words might sting a bit.* You may find an anti-pattern or two that your team is currently performing. Embrace empiricism—be transparent and honestly inspect what you are doing today. Then make the adaptations needed to get back to good Scrum practices. Don't worry, this book will help you. We've loaded it with tips, tricks, and techniques to get your Scrum teams moving forward again.

We're aware that Scrum is no longer the new and trendy framework that it used to be. In fact after over 20 years of doing Scrum, teams all over the world, companies of many sizes, and developers in particular have become jaded—and perhaps rightly so.

Bad Scrum is rampant in the software world. In many organizations, velocity is used as weapon, not a planning tool. Scope is still committed to, not managed. Product visions are unclear and value is not the center of conversations. Delivery seems like a magical event where the outcome of putting features in front of customers feels like a game of chance, not a strategic decision. Scrum masters preach self-organization, but then assign the work to the development team. Throughout this book, you'll find info about combating these anti-patterns and many others.

Worse is when companies rename their old practices with shiny new Scrum labels and immediately expect twice the work in half the time. Yet, the old patterns persist, and the empowerment promise made to developers and the commitment to quality turn out to be lies. In these circumstances, Scrum is just a bait-and-switch tactic.

So we get why some teams are upset.

Many organizations aren't getting the full benefits that Scrum—executed well—can offer. They may check a box after each Scrum event and go through the motions of Scrum. But this kind of "mechanical" Scrum is Scrum in name only, where teams use the Scrum framework without truly embodying its principles and values. Mechanical Scrum quickly degrades and becomes obsolete. Trust us, we've seen it happen.

You can rise above this by truly embracing Scrum. When you embrace self-organization, live the Scrum principles and values, and emphasize technical excellence, you empower your team to get products into the hands of customers sooner, and confirm that what the team is building is what the market actually wants. Isn't it better to invest in building products that people actually want to use?

If you want to use this wonderful framework to deliver valuable, high-quality features every sprint, read on.

Who This Book Is For

This book assumes that you're currently on a Scrum team. In Chapter 2, we provide a very brief introduction to Scrum, but after that we jump straight into the framework. Experience will help you get the most out of this book, but you can also use it to bootstrap your Scrum knowledge and get started down the path of good Scrum.

We wrote this book primarily for Scrum masters. If you're a new Scrum master, we help you avoid common traps that are easy to fall into, and give you the tools to understand the "why" behind the deeper aspects of the Scrum framework. If you're an experienced Scrum master, we provide practical tips and concrete suggestions that can help you deepen your understanding of how Scrum works—or *could* work if your organization fully embraces the Scrum principles and values.

If you manage people who are on a Scrum team, there's lots of useful info here for you, too. We present real-world examples of bad situations and provide explanations of how we've helped those teams succeed.

What's in this Book

In each chapter (starting with Chapter 3), we run through several common anti-patterns related to the topic of that chapter, and suggest ways to prevent or fix that anti-pattern on your team. At the end of each chapter is a section titled "Coach's Corner," where we provide an exercise you can try with your

Scrum at Scale

Although some of our stories and the techniques in this book are about or can be applied at scale, this book doesn't focus on ways to help you scale Scrum in environments where several development teams are working on one product. If you're considering scaling Scrum, we recommend getting really good at Scrum at a small level first, and then thinking long and hard about whether scaling is truly necessary.

team that applies to all the anti-patterns in that chapter, and which can help you narrow down the issues you're dealing with.

In Chapter 1, A Brief Introduction to Scrum, on page 1, we provide some sage advice on how to learn and explore the Scrum framework. This will give you a great refresher on Scrum and will prepare you for the upcoming chapters.

When Scrum goes bad, it isn't just the product that suffers. In Chapter 2, Why Scrum Goes Bad, on page 7, you'll see what happens when trust is lacking in an organization and empiricism isn't safe. Spoiler: Scrum doesn't thrive in this kind of environment.

But take heart! In Chapter 3, Breaking Bad Scrum with a Value-Driven Approach, on page 17 we'll explore the Scrum values. These values can promote the characteristics and behaviors that a Scrum team needs to overcome organizational dysfunction and achieve high performance. These values are really, really important. You may want to read this chapter twice.

As the "mini-CEO" of the product, the product owner plays a fundamental role in defining the vision, assessing the value, and validating the success (or failure) of the product in the marketplace. In Chapter 4, The Product Owner, on page 23, we'll look at what happens when the product owner role is misinterpreted and/or poorly performed.

Do you have a future vision of your product? If not, we'll show you how to build one in Chapter 5, The Product Backlog, on page 39. The product backlog is where Scrum teams store anything and everything that they may need for their products in the future. It's the single source of truth for the Scrum team, who uses it to plan, forecast, roadmap, and guide the direction of the product.

Chapter 6, The Development Team, on page 57 is dedicated to the folks who develop the product. The development team is a cross-functional, self-organizing team of people who can turn product backlog items into working software. Closely examine the anti-patterns we discuss in this chapter. A dysfunctional development team doesn't often deliver product.

A Scrum master must ensure that Scrum is well-understood and enacted by the Scrum team. Chapter 7, Embracing the Scrum Master Role, on page 75 explores what happens when the Scrum master doesn't act as a servant leader. Honestly, many of the anti-patterns in this book can be tied directly to a weak Scrum master. Solve these anti-patterns quickly.

Management is not the enemy. In Chapter 8, Management, on page 93, we discuss how important it is for a Scrum master to have empathy for leadership and suggest meaningful and effective ways to work with middle managers. Get this right and many of your organizational impediments can be resolved much faster than previously possible.

The sprint is often the overlooked and underappreciated Scrum event. By the end of Chapter 9, Thinking in Sprints, on page 105 you'll have a deeper understanding of the rules of the sprint and what can happen when Scrum teams violate these rules.

Sprint Planning is a complex event that can go wrong in many different ways. Chapter 10, Sprint Planning, on page 119 examines common missteps during sprint planning, including skipping product backlog refinement during the sprint. This chapter could save you hours of wasted time if you're able to adapt the way you approach this important planning event.

The development team owns the sprint backlog. If that doesn't ring true with you, Chapter 11, The Sprint Backlog, on page 131 will help change your mind. Commitment is also a big topic we'll discuss as we explore scope issues, progress, and being transparent about work during a sprint.

Did you know that you don't have to stand up during the daily scrum? This and many more earth-shattering revelations come to light in Chapter 12, Reclaiming the Daily Scrum, on page 149.

Chapter 13, Deconstructing the Done Product Increment, on page 163 covers a lot of ground. We examine the pitfalls of not having a definition of "done," why "visible" doesn't mean "transparent," and what to do when Scrum teams and the organization don't adopt the concept of done.

Did you know that the sprint review isn't a demo? Chapter 14, The Sprint Review, on page 175 covers the anti-patterns that come out when the sprint review isn't properly implemented or is facilitated poorly. Learn how to engage your stakeholders, collaborate with your customers, and get the info you need to update your product backlog and start the next sprint with the best information possible.

If you're using the "What Went Well," "What Didn't Go Well," and "What Do We Need to Change" format—STOP. Read Chapter 15, The Sprint Retrospective, on page 191 and update your retrospective practices. Continuous improvement is essential to good Scrum. A well-executed sprint retrospective generates the insights a Scrum team needs to continuously improve their process, practices, and interactions.

How to Read This Book

It would be odd for two Scrum trainers to tell you what to do. So we'll simply say, "It depends."

Just kidding.

Feel free to jump to any chapter in the book. If you're looking to learn about Scrum and the many anti-patterns that teams perform, we suggest going through the chapters in order. However, if there's an immediate problem that you want to work on, turn to the chapter related to the event, artifact, or role that contains your anti-pattern and let the improvements begin.

Online Resources

This book has its own web page[1] where you can find more information about it. Help improve this book by reporting errata, including content suggestions and typos.

Let's begin.

---

1.   https://pragprog.com/rrscrum

CHAPTER 1

A Brief Introduction to Scrum

Have you read *The Scrum Guide*™?

It *seems* like a silly question. Ryan recently asked an experienced Scrum Team this question. How could a two-year-old team not have read *The Scrum Guide*? It's only about 20 pages long, after all. Well, out of a team of nine, *only five hands went up*.

We've performed this experiment many times and have yet to see every hand go up. We encourage you to ask your team this question. It gives you a chance to learn how well your team understands Scrum, and you'll likely get some good ideas for future coaching sessions. It's also a great opportunity to have your team read *The Scrum Guide* together and discuss it.

Please read The Scrum Guide.[1] It's the universally agreed-upon definition of Scrum, and is maintained by the co-creators of Scrum—Ken Schwaber and Jeff Sutherland—who update it occasionally. Admittedly, *The Scrum Guide* is dense. We read it regularly and often debate about our different interpretations of the nuances. There are many benefits to having you and your team read and have those same debates.

Just remember that Scrum isn't a panacea. Scrum exposes all of the existing problems in an organization by making them transparent. It may bring to light problems that you didn't even know existed. There are deliberate inspection points in the Scrum events that provide opportunities to harness the brainpower of your organization to solve these problems, adapt to the changing conditions you face, and create transparency every step of the way. Scrum won't magically fix the issues it uncovers, but it does provide tools and techniques that—if applied well—can lead to success. Our goal with this book is to help ensure that you're able to use Scrum effectively in your organization.

---

1. http://www.scrumguides.org

Scrum is a powerful framework built for the complex domain of work such as software development, which is what we focus on in this book. To learn more about complex domains of work, we highly recommend that you familiarize yourself with the *Cynefin Framework*[2] or the *Stacey Matrix*.[3] They're both great ways to understand the various domains of work and can be fantastic resources for helping convince others in your organization to embrace empiricism (in other words, to be guided by experience) rather than crave certainty. Empiricism is at the core of Scrum. Every Scrum event is an opportunity to check your work and make new decisions as you learn more about the product you're creating. Initially, changing direction based on experience (empiricism) may be difficult to get people to buy into, but positive results will help you win them over.

Without further ado, here's our attempt at the world's shortest explanation of the Scrum framework. (We'll provide lots more details about these various elements throughout the following chapters.)

Joe asks:

What's the difference between a framework and a methodology?

We get this question a lot in our Scrum training classes.

A framework is a supporting structure. Scrum defines roles, events, and artifacts (more on these in a sec) but is largely silent on exactly how you should go about performing the roles and facilitating the events. A methodology, on the other hand, provides a checklist of actions to complete before moving on to the next phase or step of a process.

Because Scrum is a framework and not a methodology, it forces Scrum teams to make their own decisions within the Scrum structure. The upside is that Scrum provides an environment where you have the flexibility to find creative ways to solve complex problems and deliver great products.

A Quick Overview

Scrum is a framework that's based on empirical process control—process control that's designed to guide you by experience rather than define explicitly all of the steps up-front. Scrum was designed for complex problems. When working in a complex domain, more is unknown than known about the

---

2.   https://en.wikipedia.org/wiki/Cynefin_framework
3.   https://en.wikipedia.org/wiki/Ralph_D._Stacey

problem you're trying to solve. Since you can't plan complexity perfectly, you and your Scrum team have to leverage the three pillars of empirical process control—inspection, adaptation, and transparency—to arrive at a solution.

Here is an overview of the Scrum framework that shows, at a high level, the order of events, the roles during the Scrum events, and how the artifacts of the framework are used to make information transparent:

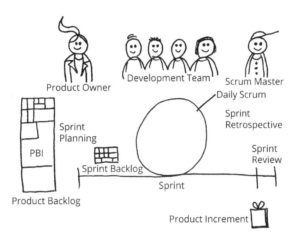

Scrum is comprised of 11 elements split into three categories:

- Roles: Each role has clear responsibilities and accountability. Together, the three roles comprise a Scrum team. Scrum teams are self-organizing and cross-functional, meaning they choose how best to accomplish their work and have all competencies and skills needed to deliver products.

    - Product owner: Is accountable for maximizing the value of the product.

    - Development team: Decides how to build the product and has all the skills necessary to build it.

    - Scrum master: A servant leader who promotes, supports, and teaches Scrum within the Scrum team and throughout the organization.

- Artifacts: These are designed to maximize the transparency of the work performed by the development team and are continually inspected and adapted during the Scrum events.

    - Product backlog: The product owner owns this artifact, which is where everything and anything that may be needed for the product (now or in the future) is stored.

- Sprint backlog: The development team owns this artifact, which contains the plan for the current sprint.

- Increment: This is a "done" and usable version of the product that's produced by the development team during a sprint.

• Events: These prescribed, time-boxed happenings are used to create regular opportunities to inspect and adapt the Scrum artifacts and to minimize the need for meetings not defined in Scrum.

- Sprint: The container event within which the other four events occur. The sprint should be one month or less in duration.

- Sprint planning: Happens at the beginning of the sprint when the Scrum team gathers and creates a plan for the sprint.

- Daily Scrum: When the development team inspects where they are in relation to the sprint goal and adapts their work plan for the next 24 hours.

- Sprint review: At the end of a sprint, the Scrum team and stakeholders gather and collaborate to inspect the increment and adapt the product backlog.

- Sprint retrospective: The last event in a sprint, where the Scrum team meets and decides how to improve in the next sprint.

People are sometimes shocked by this list. It doesn't contain many of the complementary practices that have been interpreted as required by Scrum such as user stories, sprint burndown charts, story points, velocity, etc. Although these practices may be useful in some situations to enhance empirical process control, Scrum only requires these 11 elements.

The Scrum framework can seem mechanical on its own. Many Scrum teams treat the roles, artifacts, and events as items to check off of a list during a Sprint, rather than as powerful tools for delivering products. This lack of life in the framework was likely why, in 2017, the Scrum founders added the Scrum values to The Scrum Guide: Focus, Openness, Commitment, Courage, and Respect. Although a new addition to the guide, you can find the Scrum values in early books written by Ken Schwaber, the co-creator of Scrum. The addition of them to the guide brought to light that some Scrum implementations lacked the necessary life to be successful. Here's an explanation of each value:

- Courage: A Scrum team should have the courage needed to work transparently, to do the right thing—even when it's painful—and to tackle difficult challenges.

- Focus: Everyone should be focused on the sprint goal and the desired outcome of the sprint. The product owner must be focused on value, while the development team should focus on delivery and quality under the watchful eye of the Scrum master, who's focused on the team's use of Scrum and on removing any impediment that blocks them from delivering the increment.

- Commitment: People should commit to bringing their best efforts forward and helping each other succeed.

- Respect: Scrum team members need to show respect for one another and for everyone outside the team, seeing them as capable, intelligent, and creative problem solvers who are each doing the best work they can.

- Openness: Everyone knows that bad news doesn't get better with age. Scrum teams must be open with stakeholders about all the work, challenges, and issues they encounter during a sprint.

These values infuse life into the framework and help encourage the positive behaviors that teams need to display in order to use Scrum effectively. They should be applied and promoted across an entire organization to increase the Scrum team's chances of succeeding in creating a great product.

We've only covered the bare essentials in this chapter. But don't worry, we take a deep dive into each of the 11 elements and the Scrum values throughout this book. If there's a particular aspect of Scrum that you're unclear on, feel free to jump ahead to the chapter about that element.

In the next chapter, we turn our attention to what happens to a team and an organization when Scrum isn't well-understood or properly used by development teams.

CHAPTER 2

Why Scrum Goes Bad

Scrum itself doesn't go bad—it's the ways that organizations implement it that can be problematic. We frequently see people changing the Scrum framework to fit their organization rather than the organization itself changing. Changing an organization can be slow and frustrating, but the whole point of adopting Scrum is to switch to a more efficient and empowering way of creating products, so change is a must.

We've experienced, and sometimes even promoted, many of the Scrum anti-patterns that we'll describe in this book. The root cause of these anti-patterns is typically policies that have been in place since long before the company adopted Scrum. Such longstanding policies can sometimes make what Scrum brings to light seem counterintuitive. For example, the idea of having a dedicated product owner who is fully empowered to make all decisions about a product can feel really foreign to many organizations, but having someone in that role is crucial to the success of any Scrum team.

As Scrum masters, part of our service is to the organization, and that means one aspect of our role is making sure the organization is fully embracing the Scrum way of doing things—which may require changes. Organizational change can come in many forms, such as:

- Working with HR to redefine job roles.

- Working with Finance to understand how budgeting processes impact the way teams work.

- Helping Management adopt agile leadership principles.

- Removing the divide between IT and business partners.

In order to know which change(s) your organization needs to make, you first need to understand the underlying causes of bad Scrum.

Turning Scrum into Best Practices

Ryan once worked with an organization whose Project Management Office created a 500-page Scrum manual that detailed the processes and "best" practices that *all* their Scrum teams had to follow. Not surprisingly, these "Scrum" best practices looked a lot like the old waterfall processes the company used prior to adopting Scrum. We aren't against teams creating their own practices within the Scrum framework—that's actually a good sign of a team that's working well together. But we've seen many organizations take the idea of "best" practices too far (like with the 500-page manual). A best practice is a practice you adopt and use *everywhere all the time* as the best way to do your work. But the type of work that Scrum teams do is typically too complex for any particular practice to *always* be the best approach, so there's no such thing as a best practice in Scrum.

At the other end of the "Scrum as a best practice" spectrum is the tendency to modify the Scrum framework itself. This can be very tempting, but don't do it. When a team only uses part of the framework, they lose most of the benefits of working with Scrum. What do these framework changes look like? Here are some examples:

- Treating every Scrum event as optional. We have enough meetings as it is!

- Skipping the sprint review when there isn't any work to show. I mean, it's just a demo, isn't it?

- Holding the daily scrum biweekly. Just because it's called the *daily* scrum doesn't mean we have to do it every day, right?

- Canceling the sprint retrospective in favor of getting more work done. Because who has time to improve?

- Ignoring the Scrum event time boxes. I mean, who doesn't love a 45-minute daily scrum? (Spoiler: no one loves it.)

Scrum is a collaborative framework that teams work within to help them deliver working software frequently. Your team needs to deliver an increment every sprint so they can determine whether they've met stakeholder expectations, whether customers actually want the product that they've delivered, whether they've created value at a reasonable cost and timeframe, and whether they're using the appropriate technologies. This feedback loop that the Scrum framework implements (between the Scrum team, stakeholders, and customers) is an example of risk reduction.

Along the way, you and your teams will discover that it's really hard to deliver product increments. Changes will be required at all levels of your organization, from the Scrum team all the way up and down the org chart. Changing the Scrum framework, ignoring the rules of Scrum, and simply swapping out old jargon for new-and-improved terms won't get you there.

When an organization is reluctant to fully adopt Scrum without making lots of customizations, we've found it useful to make a clear distinction between the Scrum framework and other complementary practices that the Scrum team is using. Often in our consulting engagements, we spend most of our time tearing out complementary practices in order to simplify things and firmly establish the core Scrum elements. Scrum teams should strive to get the basic elements of the framework solidly in place *before* they add any additional practices that may be needed.

Where does your team stand in terms of having the basic Scrum framework elements in place? To find out, try this simple exercise alone or with your team:

1. Write each element of the Scrum framework on a separate sticky note: Product Owner, Scrum Master, Development Team, Sprint, Sprint Planning, Daily Scrum, Sprint Review, Sprint Retrospective, Product Backlog, Sprint Backlog, and Increment.

2. Next, grab a different color sticky note and write down each complementary practice your team uses (one per sticky note), such as story points, poker planning, or sprint burndown charts.

3. Now that you have a list of the Scrum elements and a list of the complementary practices, on every sticky note, write a score from 1 (we aren't doing this at all) to 5 (we've mastered this).

4. Finally, reflect on how you can get every Scrum element sticky to a 5. Are you spending too much time and effort on complementary practices? Are any complementary practices prohibiting a Scrum element from getting to a 5?

Best practices work well for work that is repeatable or can be standardized, but Scrum is designed for solving complex problems. All too often, we cling to best practices as a way to feel like we know exactly what's going to happen. Wouldn't it be great if we could follow a 100-step process (filled with best practices) and always get the results that we expect? However, complex work doesn't play out that way. We need, instead, to be transparent both within the Scrum team and to the wider organization, to have frequent opportunities to inspect and evaluate our work, and to have the ability to make adaptations as needed. Scrum is a simple framework with 11 elements that provide a means of using empiricism (transparency, inspection, and adaptation) to your advantage. Adding complementary practices to Scrum may enhance the framework, but you must be doing Scrum well *before* you adopt any additional practices.

Lacking Goals

Want to know the best way to demotivate a development team? Keep them from seeing how their work impacts your customers. Likewise, it's demotivating for a Scrum team when they don't know how their product relates to the overall mission of the company. This misalignment of value and purpose can make it difficult for a Scrum  team to have their own clear goals that reflect larger organizational goals. This cascades all the way down to sprint goals—and without sprint goals, the development team lacks urgency and inspiration. In that situation, the developers become backlog lumberjacks: they chop through features and stories without really understanding why they're doing that work.

What does this look like in practice?

- Carrying work over across multiple sprints becomes the norm. We'll finish that PBI in the *next* sprint, right?

- Your team actually starts using a sprint goal (hurray!) but it's basically just "finish the sprint backlog" (boo!).

- Quality suffers. We don't know why we're doing the work or who it helps, so who cares how good it is?

- Stakeholders get upset. A lack of a product vision equals a vacuum of product leadership that ultimately gets filled by the development team. And there is no way for developers to magically know what customers want, especially if they do not know how their work is impacting customers.

Scrum teams work best when they are aligned with the organization's goals and customers' needs. Leadership sets the high-level goals for a company, product visions serve these goals and the customers' needs, and sprint goals keep Scrum teams aligned with the customers. When this alignment is in place, the Scrum team has purpose. Purpose is a powerful tool that can bring a team together and keep them inspired and motivated to deliver great products.

Does your Scrum team lack goals? This happens when executives fail to advertise company goals clearly or fail to communicate changes to company goals. Goals, from the organizational level cascading all the way down to a

Scrum team's sprint goal, should be measurable and customer-focused. Work with your product owner to clearly understand *why* your team is doing the work they're doing. Trace it all the way up to the company's goals and mission.

During your next retrospective, see if your team can make the connection between their sprint goal and a corporate goal. Ask the product owner and development team to reflect on the sprint goal from a recently completed sprint and have them connect this goal to the product vision, and ultimately to a corporate goal. Making these connections explicit can help the Scrum team stay focused on the impact of their work.

Taylorism Creeping Back in

We've worked in countless organizations where people hold strong beliefs about product development that aren't compatible with the proper use of the Scrum framework. These beliefs are often held both by people in various levels of management and among the people doing the work. These beliefs are often overlooked and rarely discussed because the trust needed to talk about them is lacking. To make matters more difficult, many of these beliefs are deeply rooted in corporate culture and are difficult to work through.

What kinds of beliefs, you ask? Ones that people in management and large organizations have held for a *long* time. In fact, many of these beliefs are over 100 years old. We won't bore you with the details, but in 1911, Frederick Winslow Taylor published a study called The Scientific Principles of Management,[1] which resulted in a methodology known as Taylorism. Taylorism is rooted in the idea that we can break tasks into very small, simple steps that can be analyzed, taught, and repeated. The goal was to separate workers' brains from their hands. In other words, remove the need to *think* about the work and simply give people small steps to follow to complete a task. With small steps in place, the result is predictability and compliance, not innovation.

Taylorism was designed to solve manufacturing problems that were prevalent in the industrial era (which emphasized repeatable work), and it solved those problems quite well. But when people apply the principles of Taylorism to complex work in the innovation and development space, the results are typically disastrous.

Taylorism differs *dramatically* from the Scrum way of doing things. A quick summary of the main beliefs in Scrum and Taylorism is shown in the table on page 12.

---

1.   https://en.wikipedia.org/wiki/The_Principles_of_Scientific_Management

Taylorism	Scrum
Workers only know how to do the specific tasks they've been assigned; they don't have or need a big-picture view of what their organization is trying to accomplish and are not encouraged to broaden their skill sets.	Work is performed by cross-functional teams that have all the skills they need to get the job done. These teams are supported by leadership, and high levels of trust are leveraged between leadership and Scrum teams to make decisions quickly and deliver increments of working software to customers frequently. Workers are encouraged to broaden their skill sets and collaborate.
Managers plan work without input from the people who perform the work.	Planning happens at varying levels across all the Scrum roles. Management is invited in to inspect the team's work during sprint reviews and to collaborate with the product owner, so that the team can take management and stakeholder opinions into consideration as they figure out what to do during the next sprint.
Management tries to make the work as predictable as possible by precisely managing resource utilization with exact estimates.	Scrum teams manage their time and focus as they plan their work. The development team is responsible for resource utilization. They use estimates to trigger conversations within the Scrum team and with management—not to make the work as predictable as possible.
Management optimizes workers' performance using metrics and measurements.	Scrum teams use metrics to optimize outcomes that benefit the customer.
Management uses money and rewards as primary motivators for performance. Workers are motivated to achieve rewards and avoid punishment (extrinsic motivation).	Scrum team members have a goal they are trying to achieve, the autonomy to achieve it, and a comprehensive set of skills to accomplish their goal. They also have opportunities to learn from each other. Team members are motivated to perform their work because they enjoy what they do and feel a sense of personal accomplishment (intrinsic motivation).

Table 1—Taylorism vs. Scrum

As you can see, Taylorism and Scrum are two *very* different mindsets. They are basically opposite ways of approaching work. So it's no surprise that adopting Scrum in an organization that is accustomed to the Taylorism way of doing things can be an uphill battle. Keep this info in mind when you're trying to bring people in your organization around to the Scrum way of doing things. It'll help you understand where people's opposition to Scrum practices comes from.

When Taylorism and Scrum are at odds in your organization, you'll likely see some of these signs:

- A mechanical implementation of the Scrum framework without truly embracing its principles and values.

- Scrum team members view Scrum as just new way to get micromanaged.

- No meaningful signs of collaboration between Scrum team members.

- The Scrum team is producing poor-quality increments.

- People are still being measured by how busy they are, not by the outcomes of their work.

- The Scrum team is unable to deliver increments of product every sprint.

- Reverting back to past practices—but calling them by new names.

Keep an eye out for these signs that the old ways of working are still at play in your organization. This book describes a lot of anti-patterns that occur when Taylorism and Scrum compete with each other. Adopting Scrum will require conversations about your company's culture that will give you an opportunity to create change. Take advantage of those opportunities so you can positively impact your organization and move it more toward the Scrum model, which represents the world we work in today far better than Taylorism does.

Trust is Missing

Trust is a weird thing: it's contextual, exists on a spectrum, and is very transactional. Think about your relationships. You trust some people with certain aspects of your life, but not everything. For instance, Todd and Ryan trust each other to work on this book and to co-teach a good class together—but they don't trust each other to do each other's laundry. And trust changes over time. It can take a long time to build up trust with someone, and then one misstep can wipe it out.

What does trust look like on a Scrum team?

- The product owner trusts the development team to create a done product increment by the end of every sprint.

- The development team trusts the product owner to provide them with a clear product vision.

- Development team members trust one another to do their best and support one another.

- Management trusts the Scrum team and removes any impediments to delivery.

Without trust, you can't have transparency. If the members of a Scrum team don't trust each other or an organization doesn't trust a Scrum team, then it's impossible to make the team's work and progress evident to stakeholders. Instead, people play defense: they blame one another and fail to work as a truly collaborative team.

Want to quickly make your organization trust your Scrum team? Deliver. We've found no better way to build trust than consistently delivering increments of products every sprint.

But how do you increase the likelihood that a Scrum team can work together smoothly and deliver successfully? Well, other than solving the many anti-patterns in this book, here are a few quick ideas you can try:

- Shorten your sprint length. Instead of a four-week sprint, try a one-week sprint. The development team will have fewer product backlog items to focus on, the product owner will have stakeholders in the sprint review even more frequently, and collaboration will happen in shorter intervals.

- Focus sprint planning on setting a sprint goal that has a true impact on the customer. This helps inspire the team and gives them something real to work toward.

- Use the daily scrum as an opportunity for the development team to inspect their progress toward their sprint goal. Celebrate progress and promote opportunities for Scrum team members to support and help one another. This helps increase trust within the team.

- Create opportunities for the Scrum team to collaborate with real customers. The sprint review event is perfect for this. Who better to talk about the impact of the team's work than the people who are actually affected by it?

• Introduce or reemphasize the importance of the Scrum values. If you and your team keep the Scrum values in mind, then empiricism will shine.

If you see that trust is lacking—either between your Scrum team and the rest of the organization or within the team itself—do everything in your power to find a way to build trust. We offer tips and exercises for doing so throughout the rest of this book. For Scrum to work to its full potential, trust is mandatory.

Coach's Corner

Most big organizational structures are based on Taylorism; something that has been in place for so long takes time to unwind. Scrum has been around for over 20 years, but a lot of large organizations have been around for far longer than that. Even newer organizations likely have employees who are used to the older, pre-Scrum ways of doing things.

But change *is* possible. As a Scrum master, you can unwind old policies and create new ones every day! A great way to figure out where to start (or continue) creating change in your organization is to perform this exercise, which is inspired by the liberating structure, 15% Solutions:[2]

1. Gather all the Scrum masters in your organization.

2. Discuss with them how far your organization has come in terms of transitioning to the Scrum way of doing things and how much is still left to do. If it's helpful, reference the Taylorism vs. Scrum info we presented in this chapter.

3. Have everyone in the group spend five minutes on their own answering the following question: What's within my control that I can change to get our organization 15% closer to where it needs to be?

4. Put people in groups of two to four, and have each person take three minutes to share their 15% Solution with their group. Make sure that the people who aren't sharing are actively listening and *not* giving feedback or advice.

5. Finally, have each team member spend five minutes sharing their idea(s) again—but this time encourage the other team members to ask questions and give feedback to each 15% Solution.

---

2. http://www.liberatingstructures.com/7-15-solutions/

Thinking in terms of 15% Solutions can keep people from feeling overwhelmed. Concentrating on what's within our control and finding a way to get 15% closer to where we want to be can be a powerful exercise.

In this chapter, we covered some of the old practices that Scrum often competes against in organizations. Next, we'll delve into how we can break bad Scrum by concentrating on the values and principles that influence behaviors both within a Scrum team and in the wider organization.

CHAPTER 3

Breaking Bad Scrum with a Value-Driven Approach

Knowing what we value is important. Bad Scrum thrives in environments where intent isn't clear, values are implicit instead of explicit, and old ways of working take precedence over innovation. But if you don't know the Scrum values, how can you begin to fix your Scrum? Simple: you can't. So let's take a quick tour of the Scrum values to make sure they're fresh in your mind.

Reviewing the Scrum Values

Scrum is a simple framework. There are three roles, five events, and three artifacts. Teams can get up and running very quickly. But software development is complex and so are people. When things are going well, the complexity seems manageable. But when stuff starts hitting the fan, bad things can and do happen. These difficult moments are why we need the Scrum values.

Commitment, focus, openness, respect, and courage are the five Scrum values. Understanding them can lead to better decisions, higher-quality work, and a truly collaborative environment.

These values are critical to understanding the "why" of Scrum. They act as guideposts when your team gets lost. More importantly, they drive the decisions that impact your daily work. Failing to understand them prevents your team from improving their ability to deliver value.

Here's why each value is so vital:

- Commitment can transform a team. It's a promise to yourself, your teammates, and your organization to do the very best work you can. If everyone on your Scrum team is committed to delivering a done increment of valuable product each and every sprint, you can accomplish great things together.

- Focus allows us to do our very best. Valuing focus means that we give people the time they need to think about their work. After all, creativity is hard enough without being constantly interrupted. Allowing development team members to focus just on one product, the current sprint, and the current sprint goal gives them the best chance of succeeding. Encourage the product owner to focus on the future value of the product while you, the Scrum master, focus on upholding Scrum.

- Openness is the core of transparency, which is what makes Scrum work. If the members of your Scrum team (and the people who work with your team) aren't open with each other and the wider organization, they can't solicit honest feedback or adapt their work accordingly. You need to be open and honest, even when you're struggling or there's a tough issue to address. If you aren't, transparency will suffer.

- Respect creates a feeling of safety. Being open with others can be scary and admitting when you're stuck is hard, but respect makes these actions easier. A high-performing Scrum team is built on mutual respect, and honest discussions create the safety needed to tackle difficult issues. Respect helps a team gel, grow, and learn together.

- Courage is the linchpin of the other Scrum values. It takes courage to commit, to focus amid distractions, and to be open to new ideas. And it takes courage and faith in your teammates to count on having respectful interactions when you need to discuss problems.

The Scrum values can guide you through the many obstacles and difficult situations that inevitably arise during software development projects. Without these values, your practices become rote and collaboration feels forced and mechanical. Don't let that happen to your team.

Let's think about specific ways to use the Scrum values to keep your team on track.

Using the Scrum Values Every Step of the Way

A central theme of this book is how to apply the Scrum values during the many complicated situations you'll face while playing the game of Scrum. But what do the values mean to you both as an individual and as part of a team?

When your organization first adopts Scrum, the folks on your team may have a wide range of feelings about that change. For example, someone who's used to being a hero coder may have a hard time adjusting to being equal to all the other developers. And someone who was formerly a project manager (and is now the product owner) may feel like the skills they've spent years honing may be irrelevant in Scrum. But hopefully, a lot of your team members will be enthusiastic about the many benefits that Scrum offers and will be excited to start working as a lean, mean software development team.

The Scrum values give Scrum teams a core set of values that they hold to and live by. Living these values helps team members bring their authentic selves forward and creates the alignment needed for them to do their best work. But for many teams, adopting the Scrum values isn't quick or automatic. It takes dedication and hard work for a team to establish its own identity and to embrace the Scrum values in a way that works for them.

As Scrum masters, part of our role is to help teams discover what they value and how they internalize the Scrum values. Make a point of having your team reflect on the Scrum values during sprint retrospectives or at some other time. The important thing is that these discussions happen.

Here are a few powerful questions to ask the team as they explore the Scrum values:

- Why do courage, commitment, focus, respect, and openness matter? Ask people to give examples of situations where specific values helped them.

- How do we act on the Scrum values? If your team members aren't using the values to guide their actions, they risk performing uninspired, mechanical Scrum.

- What happens when the Scrum values aren't present on our team? One example: without respect, team members may lack the courage to be open with one another.

Once you feel that your team is aligned on the Scrum values, you can use the values as a decision-making tool. Teams inevitably get stuck. Decisions about a process, tool, architecture, or team practice can get complicated quickly. As the Scrum master, try to recognize when the team is stuck and use these powerful questions to help focus the discussion and reach a consensus.

Often, the team will make a decision based on the Scrum values and move forward with its work. But sometimes, problems will arise that truly challenge the team. Your Scrum team will ignore past agreements, violate the Scrum values, and not meet their commitments. This is normal, but when it happens, you need to take the opportunity to inspect and adapt the team's practices based on this experience.

The sprint retrospective, which we discuss in detail in the last chapter of this book, is a great opportunity to explore how to help a team that's struggling with the Scrum values. This work can be difficult, but it's important to help team members come together and align toward a common goal.

After your team hits a rough patch, ask the following questions (or ones like these) during the sprint retrospective, as your team works to regain alignment and adapt its understanding of the Scrum values:

- When is it difficult to live the values of courage, commitment, focus, respect, or openness?

- What gets easier when we embrace the Scrum values?

- Which Scrum value(s) helped us the most this sprint?

- Is there a specific value that you think we especially need to work on within the team?

After this important discussion, you need to turn the insights you glean from it into actionable product backlog items for continuous improvement. That will help the team be accountable for their culture and the way they work together. Improving on how we embrace the Scrum values and making the improvements actionable is how we grow as both individuals and as a team. So let's discuss some ways to turn your insights into actions.

The Scrum Values in Action

"I wish we could talk about our small failures instead of having to wait until they're major issues."

These memorable words came from a colleague of Ryan's a number of years ago, and they still resonate with Ryan today. We were working with Scrum teams, but this colleague didn't feel safe discussing small failures with anyone.

Large issues, on the other hand, were no problem. When a big, obvious problem reared its ugly head, leadership would rally the troops and teams would work late nights and into the weekends to solve them. At the end of one of these "fire drills," the managers would talk about the team's great effort, and leadership would be pleased with the team's commitment to delivering what they promised.

The lesson: Mentioning small mistakes could get you reprimanded or blamed for causing them, whereas working late to solve major issues could get you promoted (even though these big problems could have been avoided altogether if they had been fixed when they were still small issues...)

This approach (not being transparent when small issues arise) isn't Scrum—not even a little. But it's still common, even on Scrum teams.

Ironically, being able to respond to small failures is often what makes the overhead and expense of adopting Scrum worth the cost and time it takes to get good at Scrum. But organizations where people don't feel safe discussing small issues miss out on this huge benefit. Let's use Scrum and the Scrum values to frame this idea a little more clearly.

Sprint planning, which we cover in Chapter 10, Sprint Planning, on page 119, is about figuring out which product backlog items can fit into a sprint, and then decomposing the first few stories into smaller pieces. You're intentionally making your work small so that if you do make a mistake, miss a dependency, make the wrong assumption, or flat out mess up, it's small and correctable.

The daily scrum, which we discuss in Chapter 12, Reclaiming the Daily Scrum, on page 149, is for coordinating a day's worth of work to make sure that the development team is on track to deliver on their sprint goal by the end of the sprint. This micro-planning event is all about exploring opportunities and delivering on them early, to keep the project moving forward.

During the sprint review, which is the subject of Chapter 14, The Sprint Review, on page 175, the Scrum team collaborates with stakeholders to inspect the latest increment of working software against the product backlog to see if any changes are needed, based on what the team learned during the preceding sprint. Delaying (or not holding) this event can cause the team to continue down an incorrect path.

The sprint retrospective is the perfect opportunity for the team to inspect how they did their work and come up with experiments that can help them improve in future sprints. During this event, it's essential for everyone to be able to talk about small failures and ways to improve, so that the team can advance its Scrum practices.

Scrum is designed to keep failures small and manageable, making risk management a built-in feature of the framework. If your team can't talk about its small failures openly, that increases the risk that big troubles are around the corner.

This is why openness, courage, and commitment are essential for Scrum teams. Being open about what's going on, having the courage to speak the truth to management, and being committed to delivering high-quality products are all vital to catching problems early—while they're still small.

Take time to discuss small failures with your team and encourage the great learning opportunities that they can bring. After all, these opportunities are one of the major rewards of adopting Scrum.

Coach's Corner

Given the importance of the Scrum values, you should make a point to coach your team on them regularly. Here are two ways you can help your team get more familiar with the Scrum values:

- During your next sprint retrospective, write each value across the top of a whiteboard. Then ask the team to come up with ways that they applied each value during the last sprint. You should also ask how the values were violated. Use the responses to generate a discussion about each value. Over time, this will create a common understanding about how each value applies to the team. If your team is struggling with embracing the Scrum values, you can perform this exercise during every retrospective. If, on the other hand, your team is consistently working well together, you may not need to perform it very often (though you should still do it occasionally, just to keep the values fresh in everyone's minds.)

- If your team is more action-oriented, you can try framing each Scrum value as a product backlog item in the product backlog. Here is a story format you can use to get you started: "As a __, *I want to* ____ in order to ____." Use this format to make these "value stories" actionable. For example, "As a Scrum team member, I want to show up on time to Scrum events in order to show my teammates that I respect them."

When you decide to adopt Scrum, you accept not only the practices but also the Scrum values. Now that you understand them a bit better, you can focus on applying them to your daily activities. Over time, you should see improvements not only in the quality of the product your team is building, but also in how your team members interact with one another.

We're ready to turn our attention to the various Scrum roles, events, and artifacts. We're going to start with the product owner, who defines the team's vision and validates that what the development team delivers is actually what customers and stakeholders want. This role is vital because, without a clear vision, the team will lack direction and won't understand why they're building their product. In the next chapter, you'll learn how commitment and focus help a product owner determine the best direction for a product.

The Product Owner

Manager: *What do you mean the site is down?*

In the United States, Cyber Monday is one of the largest online shopping days of the year. If your site is down on Cyber Monday, you're losing money—a lot of it. The manager who made the comment at the beginning of this chapter worked for a worldwide retailer and was expecting a big holiday season for online sales. The website needed to be live and taking orders for the retailer to hit the forecasted financial targets. Learning that the site had crashed right before Cyber Monday was not a great way to start the day.

Todd started working with this company right after their Cyber Monday crash. He heard stories from development team members about competing interests between product owners. In talking to the business analysts, Todd found they were often stalled in their ability to make scope-based decisions, sometimes waiting days or even weeks to meet all four product owners for approval. Yes, you read that correctly: there were four product owners for one product even though Scrum stipulates a single product owner for a product.

The issues made a lot of sense. There were seven development teams led by four product owners. These product owners were all focused on getting their areas of the application ready for release. They initially created a road map outlaying scope, schedule, and budget. But that plan took a back seat to shouting matches between the product owners, who couldn't agree on what to work on next. Nobody on the development teams truly knew where the product was going because it seemed to be moving in four different directions. Without a vision, the loudest voice (or the highest paid person) often filled the product leadership void.

For the company, this was an intense time and one for which it still bears scars today. The competing interests of the product owners were devastating. The development teams were not collaborative—in fact they were often at odds due to the many different directions the four product owners were trying to take them.

As Scrum masters, we work within our organizations to make sure that people understand the product owner's role. A product owner must be empowered to be the final decision maker in order to bring the most value to our customers. We need to ensure that the organization understands why this is so important and that management gives the product owner the necessary authority. We need to tackle situations like our four product owners story above, and bring to light the flaws in that approach.

You work side by side with the product owner, helping to find new ways to be agile and successful. This may include suggesting ways to make the product backlog transparent, facilitating conversations between the PO and the development team, teaching new techniques for interacting with stakeholders, helping the PO understand their role on the Scrum team, or assisting in being transparent to the team and stakeholders about a value hypothesis the PO has formed.

Here are some important facts about the product owner role for you to keep in mind as you read this chapter:

- The PO role should be performed by *one* person per product, not a committee.
- The PO manages and is responsible for the product backlog.
- The PO works relentlessly to maximize the value of what the development team is working on by ordering the product backlog.
- The PO is in charge of creating and maintaining the product vision.
- The PO uses Scrum as a catalyst to inspect the product and adapt its direction based on customer and stakeholder feedback.
- The PO keeps tabs on the marketplace and adapts the product with it.
- The PO works with stakeholders to gather opinions and ideas, but is empowered to make final decisions.

In this chapter, we'll explore the product owner anti-patterns illustrated by our Cyber Monday fiasco as well as others you should be aware of—and how to fix them. Our retail friends learned the hard way that a committee of product owners fails miserably. Hopefully you can use the lessons in this chapter to avoid similar situations in your workplace.

Many Product Owners, One Product

Many companies decide to give many people different pieces of the product owner role. Organizations often do this because that's what they did in the past when they used waterfall practices. They believe there isn't a single person in the organization who knows all the domains necessary to develop a product, nor anyone who has all the skills to work with development teams, stakeholders, and customers. (Those may also be separate duties in reporting structures.) So the product owner role gets split across multiple people to ensure each gets a say in how the product is built.

The product owner committee comes to the table with competing interests: technical, departmental, customer, political, organizational, etc. Eventually this leads to debates about what to build next. Each product owner has his or her own interests in mind and it's often difficult to get anyone to admit that an idea other than their own is most important. These stalemates get escalated up the org chart until someone with a big enough title gets tired of all the noise and makes a snap decision. These games take precious time which often leads to waste, turmoil, and creating products that no one wants.

You may also experience multiple product owners "owning" their particular team or area of a product within the bounds of a single product. The segregated product owners become isolated doing what they want, and as a result, there's no holistic view of what the product should be. This will result in an incohesive product for your users and likely a disjointed architecture laden with technical debt.

With one and only one product owner, the development teams know what work is truly important for the product and what they should be focused on. There is a holistic view, both within the Scrum team and to stakeholders, of where the product is now and where it's heading in the future because there is one person guiding it. The sole product owner gathers stakeholder and customer feedback and incorporates potential changes into the product backlog. And decision making isn't stalled by competing interests.

Does having multiple product owners on a single product sound familiar? We've been through this many times and know the pain that it can cause.

It's important for you to work with your organizations to show how vital it is that a product owner *must* be a single person who listens to stakeholders and customers and then makes decisions centered around the overall value of the product.

If you're dealing with a product owner committee (or the prospect of one), do everything you can to change that. Share the story at the beginning of this chapter with management to help them understand the problems such a committee will cause. More than once, we've seen platforms crash because of competing interests or disparate functionality and the downstream problems that ensued. It takes the Scrum value of courage to approach this issue with management and the multiple product owners. But trust us: this is a cause worth fighting for.

Something we find to be useful in this situation is to trace the money. Find out who owns the budget and has final say on all decisions—that person is the real product owner. Have a conversation with them highlighting the difficulties caused by having multiple product owners, and explain why having a single product owner is a better approach. By tracing the money, you'll find the right person to have this conversation with.

The Part-time Product Owner

"Where's the product owner?" We've asked this question many times while working with Scrum teams, and you probably have, too. It's frustrating. The dev team wants to keep working, but they need answers from the product owner about scope. This is a common symptom of having a product owner who is only part-time.

So how do part-time product owners come to be? When the product owner role is first explained in an organization, most executives and project managers perceive it as an almighty and threatening position. The term "product owner" implies overarching ownership of a product, but traditionally, ownership of a product is spread across various roles. This consolidation of ownership can feel threatening to some people in management who are comfortable with the way things have been done in the past.

We frequently see this initial negative reaction to the PO role in companies where the role is a new concept. The skill set is unique and unlike anything that has previously existed in many organizations. Management's natural inclination is to make it a part-time job that's added to the duties of someone with lots of decision-making authority. That's the easy thing to do: Rather than cutting through HR red tape to create a new role or seemingly diminishing the management responsibilities of a bright executive, it becomes an added responsibility for someone. That person becomes a part-time product owner.

Another way a part-time product owner can emerge is if a person on the Scrum team discovers that he or she has in effect *become* the product owner because no one else has authority to do the job. This can happen when management doesn't explicitly name a product owner—and they may not know that they need to. Unfortunately, this default product owner is undoubtedly way too busy to actually do much of the work required of a PO.

The part-time product owner makes every attempt to be there for the Scrum team, but the 10% of time allocated for that role drops quickly to 5%. This person still has a day job plus this new PO gig. The product owner makes it to sprint reviews and is sometimes thrilled and sometimes surprised by what he sees or hears. Sprint retrospectives just aren't as important as budgeting meetings, executive reviews, or putting out personnel fires. Attending the first half hour of sprint planning is all he can afford, but the team's got this, right?

This isn't a recipe for success. The Scrum master and development team often fill this product ownership vacuum. With a part-time PO, you're deciding that it makes sense to ask developers to decipher what's the next most valuable thing to put into the product, answer all the "when will it be done" questions from eager stakeholders, manage scope, and keep the product backlog up to date.

You don't want developers doing this kind of work. They should focus on figuring out how to deliver high-quality products. A development team that's distracted by PO-type work is an impediment that you need to address.

Having a part-time product owner hurts everyone. Stakeholders need a single person who is available to them. The team needs a person who they can have conversations with and who manages the product backlog. Customers need someone focused on maximizing the value of what is delivered to them. It's a full-time job. If the product owner role isn't one person's single focus, your customers will pay the price.

The products that you're building are adding value to your company and keeping it in business. The product owner is the single most important person on a Scrum team when it comes to making sure customers are satisfied. Is keeping your company in business only worth a portion of someone's time?

To combat Part-time Product Owner Syndrome, think of the product owner as an Agile product manager. Grab the existing product owner and, together, brainstorm what duties an agile product manager should perform in your organization and with customers who are outside the bounds of the Scrum framework. Here are a few possible examples:

- Evaluating competitor products
- Assessing customer information
- Building a road map
- Managing the budget
- Implementing value-based metrics
- Gathering stakeholder opinions

Discuss the duties you come up with, and note which ones the PO isn't able to complete because of their time constraints. Present this information to whomever manages the part-time PO. (Make sure the PO is with you and is actively involved in this meeting.) Create urgency around the need for a full-time product owner by discussing all the activities that aren't being addressed because of the time constraints your part-time PO faces.

The Proxy Product Owner

When your company adopts Scrum, upper management may think about the product owner role like this:

> The product owner manages the product backlog. That sounds like something a business analyst should do, right? Sure, it comes with a little more responsibility, but people in the organization might freak out if we adopt the term "product owner." We can make product backlog management the person's sole purpose, and other duties such as managing the budget will remain the way we do them now. If we give up control of the money, what happens to our job?

> Let's repurpose the project manager or business analyst role and call this new role the "product backlog manager." We'll outline our higher-level initiatives, have weekly status meetings, track the return on investment, and manage the budget the way we do now in different corners of the organization. After all, aren't the VP roles in place for those kinds of duties?

The product backlog manager simply writes the requirements that stakeholders provide and ensures that the team delivers exactly what's listed in the backlog. There's even a chance that HR has created a role with the official title of "Product Owner." The responsibilities defined in the HR document might read like that of a glorified business analyst or a product manager. Yet, the role is stripped of the responsibilities and accountabilities that a product owner needs to be successful.

Sometimes the issue is simple: The organization or product owner just doesn't understand Scrum. If that's the case, now is a great time to dust off your teaching boots and teach the PO and/or organization what the product owner role entails. Focus on the clear accountabilities of each Scrum role and why it's imperative that the product owner be given all the capabilities and ownership that he needs to maximize the value of what the development team is working on.

Joe asks:

What if we measure Product Backlog health?

When an organization implements a product backlog health metric, it signals that a proxy product owner exists. Organizations often implement this "metric" as a way to gauge whether the proxy PO is doing his job appropriately. People in management often believe that by creating this kind of metric, they can tell whether a development team has what they need in the product backlog to appropriately plan sprints.

"Healthy" is a red herring anyway. If you want to know if your product owner is doing his job, measure the value delivered. But if your management team is *insisting* on some kind of product backlog metric, look at transparency. In Scrum, transparent doesn't mean "visible," it means "well-understood." During the next sprint review, ask the development team and stakeholders to discuss what the product vision is and how the product backlog supports that vision. After 30 seconds of blank stares, ask the PO to step up and walk through the product backlog and discuss how it ties back to vision and value.

If your project doesn't have a fully empowered product owner who has a holistic view of the product-development effort, including financials, the proxy product owner will make ill-informed decisions on the contents and order of the product backlog. Stakeholder priorities, while important, shouldn't necessarily determine the order of items in the product backlog. There may be more valuable things to work on.

It's important for a product owner to know financial and return-on-investment information about the project so that he can have informed discussions with stakeholders. A proxy product owner often doesn't have budgetary information. He is often put in tough spots when having conversations with stakeholders about the product backlog's contents and order. It's hard for the PO to push back when he doesn't have numbers to back up his opinions.

As you can see, a proxy product owner won't cut it and can doom a product. So what can you do if you're working with a proxy product owner? Discover the de facto product owner by asking a simple question: Who do we have to talk to in order to get more money to fund another sprint? Usually you won't need more money, but it's helpful to know who makes that call. (This is similar to our advice earlier in this chapter: Trace the money.)

As a Scrum master, it's important to help your product owner gain more authority. Once you know who can approve more money (a.k.a. the decider), it's time to go have a talk. By meeting with your PO and the decider, you can help instigate some changes. Ask this decider—who's often very busy—to attend the Scrum events and product refinement sessions. We need decision makers front and center, right?

This person will likely push back due to time constraints and a jam-packed calendar. This is your opportunity to suggest that the PO can take on a more active role in decision making. Be sure not to have this conversation in a bubble: Bring your product owner with you. Advocate for decentralized decision making and quantify the amount of time and money that's wasted by waiting for decisions. This will help highlight the importance of the product owner role.

The Commander in Chief

We've described situations where product owners aren't given the proper time or authority to fulfill their role properly. But the opposite can be bad, too: A product owner who wields *too much* power and doesn't listen to anyone else.

Here's what that looks like:

> The product owner is an almighty being who doesn't collaborate because he is the single decision-making authority. The development team is expected to obey this person's every command and the team's input is not welcome. The Scrum master makes sure the development team doesn't deviate whatsoever from the product owner's orders.

> During rare meetings with stakeholders, the product owner describes how things are going to be and what is happening. It's purely a status meeting and no input is asked for because the direction of the product and features are determined by the product owner, and the stakeholders will just complicate decision making. Sprint reviews are for the product owner to approve or reject the results of the sprint; stakeholders are not required nor invited.

> During sprint planning, the product owner arrives with a goal and has prefilled the sprint backlog based off of a velocity he has set. The event is simply held to create order for the next sprint and tell the team what to do. The product owner often questions estimates of product backlog items because the tasks sure seem easier than the development team's estimates indicate. When the sprint is underway, the product owner attends the daily scrum to get a status from each team member and to make sure that the Scrum master has them working at full

capacity. The development team doesn't deviate from the plan outlined by the product owner in the sprint, even if that means sacrificing quality.

If these scenarios made you cringe because you live them every day, don't fear–there's hope even in these situations! Perhaps we need to look at the "Commander in Chief" PO a little differently.

Being a product owner can mean being lonely, and that might be what's causing this controlling behavior. Product owners have an immense amount of pressure on them: stakeholders have high expectations, development teams need clarity and support, and customers are demanding. Coupled with the fact that this might be a new role for the person or the company, the product owner could feel really scared and stressed. As a Scrum master, you should partner with the product owner by helping him build the tool set he needs to be successful. And sometimes, you might be able to help just by asking the PO, "Are you okay?"

Sometimes POs just need a breather

by: Todd Miller

While I've spent a majority of my Scrum career working as a Scrum master, I've been a PO three times and I've learned a lot from those experiences. It can be a stressful, lonely job. I'll never forget a particular day that I was really struggling with stakeholders: I was involved in several extremely tense conversations that resulted in screaming matches between stakeholders who eventually started screaming at me, too. As I left the meeting with them and walked past the development team, I was barraged with questions about product backlog items. I have to admit that, because I was in a terrible mood, I wasn't very gracious or helpful to them.

Later that same day, I received an invite for a late afternoon meeting with a few Scrum masters. I cringed at accepting it, as I anticipated that another missile was heading in my direction. I walked into the meeting room, sat down, and asked what they needed. To my surprise, they asked me what *I* needed and asked if I was okay. Turns out they simply wanted to make sure I was doing alright. We ended up just chitchatting and talking about sports. It gave me a chance to take a deep breath and decompress, which I sorely needed. It was awesome!

So if your PO seems really frazzled or grumpy, ask him how he's doing. A little empathy and understanding can go a long way toward making him feel less stressed and alone.

It's important for the product owner to take a collaborative approach with stakeholders, team members, and customers. If they instead act as a commander-in-chief, there will be little transparency around decision making, which in turn will cause the product backlog to lack transparency. Without transparency into the product backlog, the product owner may end up adapting the product backlog without technical or stakeholder input. This lack of transparency leads to a product backlog that's not ordered in a way that contributes to the success of the project.

As a Scrum master, you need to be willing to confront a product owner who has let the power and accountability of the role go to their head. But at the same time, don't *assume* that that's what is taking place: First, try asking your PO if he's okay and how you can better support him.

The Scrum Master + Product Owner

Some companies think they can get away with having one person perform the roles of Scrum master *and* product owner. Folks in management might say, "We don't have room/budget for *two* new positions so let's combine those responsibilities into a single role: Scrum master + product owner." They might even want to combine other positions into this role, too, such as project manager, architect, or even developer.

When push comes to shove, which role will they choose? Will they revert to their Scrum master accountabilities or will the product owner win out? Either way, the Scrum team will lose out on critical interactions that need to happen during sprints.

Here are the kinds of things that Scrum masters commonly discuss with development team members, stakeholders, and management:

- Development team: Upholding Scrum and ensuring that the team is optimized for empirical process control.

- Stakeholders: Creating an understanding of the complex domain of work and showing them how necessary it is to have empirical process control.

- Management: Collaborating on the organizational changes that are necessary for Scrum to succeed.

By contrast, here are the kinds of things that product owners should discuss with those same folks:

- Development team: The vision and direction of the product and how the product owner has translated that vision and direction into the product backlog.

- Stakeholders: Collaborating and keeping actively engaged with the direction of the product.

- Management: Working through the budgeting process.

Notice that these conversations are wildly different, and the various topics require totally different approaches. For example, take the conversations with management: If you are speaking to them about the budgeting process, you would use very different techniques than you would if you were proposing organizational changes. A single person can't effectively focus on both types of conversations.

What's missing from the table is the interactions that a Scrum master and product owner should be having with *each other*. There are several important interactions that a product owner and Scrum master need to have but can't if they are the same person. The product owner/Scrum master will have nowhere to turn when they need help and the product will suffer as a consequence.

A Scrum master serves the product owner in a multitude of ways. Here are a few examples:

- Facilitating interactions between the product owner and the development team.

- Helping the product owner identify and work with stakeholders.

- Working with the product owner to find ways to do proper product backlog management.

- Finding ways to make the product backlog transparent to the dev team and stakeholders.

- Teaching Scrum to the product owner.

- Coaching the product owner on agile product management.

Product owner is a full-time job that requires attention to many things outside the bounds of Scrum. A product owner is an agile product manager who evaluates the market and internal corporation with an eye on value maximization. The PO works with stakeholders to keep them informed while gathering their opinions about the direction of the product. They collaborate with the development team to help them understand the direction of the product and pave a path to get there. He creates the vision, road maps, and release plans; manages the budget, evaluates total cost of ownership, estimates return on investment, and so on.

With all of this work to do, there's no way a product owner can complete these tasks *and* the tasks expected of a Scrum master. To make people aware of this problem, try this activity (it helps to have friends for this exercise, so grab some other Scrum masters):

Think about the Scrum master role and brainstorm every task someone in that role may perform during a sprint, and create a sticky note for each task.

Once you've exhausted this list, take a break. When you return, move to the product owner role and do the same thing with different color sticky notes to differentiate between the roles. Then look at what you've created and ask:

- Are there any similarities in work?
- Are there any conflicts of interest caused by performing both roles?
- Can one person do all of these tasks?
- What and/or who may suffer if one person tries?

Now walk through the Scrum values and ask if it's really possible to focus on both roles and the work that needs to be done for each role during a sprint. Can you truly commit to performing this work at high level? Will you be open enough with the Scrum team to admit that you're struggling? Will you show the courage to admit when you don't know what to do next? Do you have enough respect for the customers and stakeholders to stop performing both roles if product delivery is suffering?

If you can't honestly answer yes to these questions, as much as it may hurt, advocate for your role (or the person assuming both of these roles) to be split into two roles.

Not Having a Clear Vision

Here's what can happen when a product owner doesn't have a clear and well-known product vision to guide their decision making:

Nobody in the organization, not even the Scrum team, knows why the heck they're building this product, but they've been doing it for years and have spent a lot of money, blood, sweat, and tears on it. The product owner works with the stakeholders and customers, then puts those interactions into the product backlog and orders them, but with no clear rhyme or reason. There's no strife or unhappiness as high-quality work is being delivered, but you notice a lack of energy and excitement around the product. Sprint reviews are like a library, interactions with stakeholders are dry and focus on just the product backlog items they care about that were delivered. There's no discussion of the overall direction of the product and what value the future might hold.

In a retrospective, the development team brings up the fact that sprints are beginning to feel like a hamster wheel: They just keep going and going with no end in sight. There doesn't seem to be an end goal or objective, just more work to do.

What is the vision for the product you're working on right now? It should be circulating in your head like the lyrics of an '80s Madonna song. Without a product vision and an accompanying measurable outcome, it's hard for anyone to give feedback on how a product can be successful. This can lead to a product owner who frequently changes his mind about where the product should be heading or what the definition of "value" is for this project. The PO may even start taking orders from stakeholders, trying to appease their every demand, which, as we've discussed, is *not* the way things should work in Scrum.

If your team doesn't have a clear product vision, then creating such a vision should be the product owner's top priority. Work with the PO to find a way to create the vision, which is the overarching direction of a product. Having a clear vision lends itself to more in-depth conversations with stakeholders, gives the development team a clear understanding of what success looks like, and provides guardrails for every decision the product owner makes.

Measurements that can validate the vision's success are an absolute necessity. If these measurements indicate that the team isn't succeeding, then perhaps the vision needs to be adjusted—or maybe it's no longer worth pursuing. The product owner needs quantifiable ways to determine whether the team is succeeding in achieving the vision, as well as whether the vision is even still worth it.

Consider that the single greatest way to motivate a development team is to let them see the impact that their work has on the world. If a product owner provides a clear product vision with outcomes, measurements, and metrics, that impact will be clearly visible to the team and the organization. This can improve morale and prove that the financial investments the organization has made in the product were worthwhile.

If your product lacks a clear product vision, get started yesterday with your product owner to create one. Be sure to solicit input from all team members and stakeholders. If you're having a tough time deciding where to start, you can start with a single word, as we explain in the following sidebar. Once everyone has a clear sense of where the product is heading, they'll be more motivated and engaged in creating a great product.

The one-word pitch method is described in Daniel Pink's book *To Sell is Human*.[1] It's one of many methods you can suggest for working with your product owner to create a vision. There are many other good ones as well,

---

1. https://www.danpink.com/books/to-sell-is-human/

The One-Word Pitch

Does your Scrum Team lack a product vision or are they having a hard time nailing down what that product vision is? Start by finding a way to describe your product in single, inspiring word (commonly referred to as a one-word pitch).

Here's an example. Let's view Scrum as a product and look deep into its value proposition: developing a high-quality, potentially shippable product increment in 30 days or less. The product owner decides whether to ship this increment, but it's ready to go thanks to the hard work of the development team.

If we were to choose a single word as a rallying cry for Scrum, something that everybody could get behind, how about the word "effectiveness?" Consider the focus this word can create for your team. If we view all of our Scrum practices through the lens of "effectiveness," we can generate a list of potential improvements we can work toward as a team.

such as Roman Pichler's *Product Vision Board*[2] or the Product Vision Box from the book *Innovation Games*.[3] Experiment with various methods and find what's right for your particular situation. And be sure to remind the product owner that the vision might change. The PO should frequently validate the vision against the metrics that accompany it, and should regularly revisit the vision to make sure it's still relevant.

Coach's Corner

The product owner is accountable for maximizing the value of what the development team is working on. This person is the single decision-making authority regarding what gets built next. The PO works tirelessly to represent stakeholders and facilitate conversations between all the customers who use and consume the products the team delivers. Product owners explore the minds of the customers. They work with development teams to consider their opinions and understand the technical implications of each decision. All of this is stored in the product backlog that they meticulously manage and order.

For the product owner to be successful, he must be empowered to make all of this happen. This includes owning the budget, managing scope, and evaluating return on investment. It's important that everyone in the organization understands why the product owner role is so vital in Scrum, and what could happen if that role were downgraded. Many organizations struggle with

---

2.   https://www.romanpichler.com/tools/vision-board/

3.   https://www.innovationgames.com/

defining and empowering the product owner. Depending on the organization's maturity, it might take a while for the product owner to be appropriately empowered.

How can you bring attention to the importance of this role in your organization? Work with your product owner to understand the depth of their interactions with stakeholders, the development team, customers, and management. Work together to create a Product Owner interaction map:

1. On a whiteboard, create four quadrants. Label them "Stakeholder," "Customer," "Development Team," and "Management" (respectively).

2. On individual sticky notes of the same color, answer this question: "What interactions is the product owner having with this group right now?". Place each sticky note in the appropriate quadrant. An example might be placing a sticky labeled "product backlog refinement" in the development-team quadrant.

3. On different color sticky notes, answer this question: "What interactions is the product owner *not* having (or not allowed to have)?" Again, place each sticky note in the appropriate quadrant. These items are impediments that are preventing your product owner from making value-based decisions. Why aren't those interactions happening? What is the first course of action you can take to change this? In other words, what is the first impediment we can remove?

It's up to you to figure out how to take action on these impediments and create change.

We've taken a look at the product owner role and seen some of the consequences of this role not being elevated to what it needs to be. Next, we'll look at a subject that's closely related: the product backlog. In this artifact, you may very well see symptoms of the anti-patterns we discussed in this chapter.

CHAPTER 5

The Product Backlog

Ryan gives a lot of keynotes at conferences all around the world and has a series of product backlog-related questions that are fun to ask, especially when there are a lot of product owners in the audience. He starts with a simple question: "How many of you have a product backlog?" The audience chuckles and the majority of people raise a hand in the air.

Next question: "How many of you have a feature, requirement, task, or bug in your product backlog that's older than three months?" The laughter fades and a serious vibe falls over the room. The majority of hands stay up.

"Alright, how about older than six months?" A few hands drop, but most stay up and people start looking at each other, realizing what's next.

"Okay, one year? Two years? How about a PBI that's older than three years?" Normally we stop there, but recently a gentleman kept his hand up until Ryan got to *nine years.* Honestly, Ryan was stunned and stopped the keynote. He asked the AV folks to bring the lights up and give this guy a mic: Ryan had to hear what had languished for nine years in a backlog.

Turns out the guy was in the financial industry and had a mainframe change to make.

> **Ryan:** *Sir, you're never going to make that change.*
>
> **Gentleman:** *No, no—we **have** to make this change.*
>
> **Ryan:** *Really? But it's been **nine years!***

A product backlog is everything a Scrum team knows about their product and what they intend to build and deliver at any given time. It's the roadmap, product vision, and execution plan. Competitors would love to get their hands on it, but only if the Scrum team has built it well.

Many product owners (and Scrum teams, for that matter) are hesitant to treat the product backlog as a living, changing document—which is exactly what it should be. Instead, they tend to think of it as an unchangeable list of things that *must* be completed—so they never remove uncompleted items, even if those PBIs have been languishing for years. Too many years of 400-page requirements documents and painful change-order processes keep many POs from refining and changing their product backlogs.

As a Scrum master, you'll spend a lot of time encouraging cuts and edits to product backlog items. Be patient. It isn't always easy for your product owner to let go of their best-laid plans and clever feature ideas.

In this chapter, we break down the many anti-patterns that ruin product backlogs. We will make sure you know how to support your product owner and create a product backlog that serves your development team and stakeholders well.

One Product, Many Product Backlogs

Ever seen a bug backlog? Yep, some Scrum teams create a separate backlog just for bugs. How about a technical-debt backlog? This one is a favorite of Ryan's from past coaching experiences: The Backlog of Broken Promises and Crushed Dreams, where every story we promised to deliver—but didn't—went to die. Crazy right? Unfortunately, it's not uncommon for Scrum teams to have multiple backlogs, especially on products that involve multiple Scrum teams.

When a product-development effort requires many development teams, the product owner often needs to delegate the task of refining the product backlog. In that situation, allocating each team their own separate product backlog might seem like the right thing to do. But in our experience, going down that path only leads to tears. When teams working on a single product have separate product backlogs:

- There's no holistic view of what needs to be accomplished, so the teams will start to diverge, leading to a product that's no longer cohesive–and possibly not even functional.

- Each team will construct their product backlog in their own way, rendering the overall product vision and goals useless.

- The underpinning architecture won't be consistent across teams, leading to technical debt and the need to rework features that aren't coherent.

- Dependencies between teams won't be considered, resulting in blame and conflict.

- Trying to integrate all of the different teams' work will add unnecessary complexity and time to sprints.

- No single team is accountable to stakeholders for the quality and value of the product.

Bottom line: *The product backlog is the single source of truth for every kind of work in Scrum.* There should only be one product owner and one product backlog on a product-development effort, regardless of the type of work or number of teams. Having one product backlog provides a holistic view of the future of the product. It creates cohesion regardless of the number of development teams that are working on the project. A single product backlog results in better conversations with stakeholders and clearer increment inspections during sprint reviews.

What do you do if you have multiple product backlogs? Your top priority should be to work with the product owner to help them create a *single* clear, well-understood vision of the product. Here are some techniques we recommend for starting the consolidation process:

1. Work with your product owner to gather every product backlog. This sounds a little silly, but there are likely many spreadsheets, notebooks, and napkins in your organization with important product information and backlog items. Check with the development team(s). They probably have lists of technical debt and "things we intend to do later," captured somewhere, that should also be included in the product backlog.

2. Ask the product owner to merge all of these lists into a single product backlog. The new backlog will be sprawling and seem overwhelming at first, but that's okay. You're about to prune it into something more manageable.

3. Delete anything that's older than six months, as you likely won't ever do the work for those features. And if that work is important, it will reappear via feedback from customers and stakeholders. Understandably, your PO may be really nervous about truly deleting any PBIs. But trust us, it's better for everyone in the organization to axe PBIs that are old and stale. The PO may be tempted to create a separate list of "deleted" PBIs "just in case," but as we discuss in the next section, that's a bad idea. The product backlog (singular!) should be the one and only source of truth for the project.

4. Group similar items together and help your product owner create new product backlog items, if needed. Refine and rework these items as you merge them together to create a unified product backlog.

5. Help the product owner order the newly built product backlog. Discuss what needs to be worked on next in order to deliver the most value in the next sprint.

6. Facilitate a product backlog refinement session with the Scrum team(s). Helping the team(s) re-establish a holistic vision of the product is important. A refinement session or two can help get everyone back on the same page and allow them to see what has changed now that all of the work is visible.

7. Have your product owner share the updated product backlog during the next sprint review.

Joe asks:
Who can update the product backlog?

The product owner is solely accountable for the state of the product backlog. However, other people may update it at the product owner's discretion. But make sure the PO is cautious about sharing this power: If several people can edit the product backlog, the result can end up being a jumbled mess. Work with the product owner to find the appropriate dynamic for your situation.

Too Many (or Too Few) PBIs

Product owners get nervous when you suggest that some of their product backlog items should be deleted. Really nervous. Sometimes they'll agree to cut the items from the product backlog...and then paste them into a *secret* product backlog, just in case. Of course, we know that there can be only one product backlog, so the PO having a separate, secret product backlog is inherently a bad idea.

An overgrown product backlog is hard to navigate, which makes it difficult to get back to the roots of your vision and see the items that will bring it to fruition. This causes communication to break down both within the Scrum team and with stakeholders, because it's impossible to gauge your progress and where you will be in the near-term and long-term future.

The opposite issue, a product backlog that lacks substance, is equally dangerous. A shortage of product backlog items leaves teams scrambling during sprint planning because there's no future for the product owner to discuss with stakeholders. Having a nearly empty product backlog is like going to the grocery store when you don't have a list—and you're hungry. You'll leave the store with whatever intrigued your stomach, but with no clear meal plan for the days ahead.

So how many product backlog items should you have? Just enough to define a short-term, mid-term, and long-term future for your product:

- Short-term items (a.k.a. stories) should have the most detailed requirements. It's good to have two to three sprints worth of such items that are ready for the development team to bring into a sprint. These items should contain enough detail that the development team feels confident bringing them into a sprint, but not *so* much detail that there's little flexibility in the outcome.

- Mid-term items (a.k.a. features) are things that will be accomplished 3-6 months from now. They should have enough detail for the development team to know the direction that the product is heading. Invest minimal time here. Remember, PBIs are emergent—things will change before you get to these items. Rough estimates and sizing are perfectly fine for these PBIs.

- Long-term items (a.k.a. epics) can be vague. They should describe what the product might contain in the distant future. These items are too large to be finished within a single sprint, are often unclear, and will need multiple refinement sessions to become actionable.

So what do you do if your product backlog is too crowded, too sparse, or doesn't clearly define the future of your project? There's no panacea for successfully refining your product backlog, but here are some tips.

Make Product Backlog Refinement Fit Your Situation

There's no single, prescriptive technique that you can use to ensure that your product backlog is in good shape for future sprints. Product backlog refinement—where the development team and product owner collaborate to add details, estimates, order, and/or decomposition to the product backlog—can occur daily, weekly, or once a sprint. The exact timing doesn't matter as long as the refining gets done.

It's perfectly acceptable for the product owner to delegate and ask the development team to refine items informally as needed. You may also choose to make refinement a formal event that occurs on a regular schedule within your sprint. No matter what technique and schedule you choose, inspect and adapt during sprint retrospectives to find out what works best for your Scrum team.

 Joe asks:

Isn't this process called product backlog *grooming*?

Though you may still hear that phrase used by some Scrum teams, the authors of *The Scrum Guide* changed "product backlog grooming" to "product backlog refinement" several years ago. The term "grooming" has extremely negative connotations in some parts of the world. "Product backlog refinement" sounds more professional. It's important to keep up with changes like these so you don't unintentionally offend anyone. That's one of the many reasons we recommend reading *The Scrum Guide* regularly.

Don't involve everyone

Many people think that, in self-organizing development teams, everybody needs to be involved in everything, but that may not be true for your team's product backlog refinement sessions. If it feels like a waste of time to involve everybody, then don't. As the Scrum master, you can talk to the development team about who should attend a given refinement session, and have them decide. It's important that everyone on the development team understands what's in the product backlog, especially prior to sprint planning. That doesn't necessarily mean everybody has to be involved in refinement all the time. Trust them to talk to each other.

Estimate only when necessary

The later you estimate, the closer you'll be to the work and the more relevant that estimate will be. Some people argue that an accurate estimate is impossible and a waste of time when working in a complex profession like software development. While it's rarely possible to estimate *exactly* how things will play out, creating estimates is still worthwhile for two key reasons:

- Estimates allow the product owner to decipher the return on investment of a PBI when weighing the expected value of a feature against the forecasted effort that will be involved in building it.

- Estimates provide the development team with details that can help them determine what might need to happen to bring the item into a sprint. For example, it can help them determine whether a single PBI could (or should) be split into multiple items. Conversations about the work are often more important than the actual estimate.

The act of estimating helps the Scrum team understand a product backlog item. It's about the conversations that are sparked by the process, not the actual estimate. When and how you estimate product backlog items is entirely up to your team and should fit your situation. As a Scrum master, it's important to know multiple estimating techniques that you can teach your team. A good resource for learning effective agile estimation techniques is Predicting the Unpredictable by Johanna Rothman.[1]

Don't get too far ahead

If you're refining product backlog items that the development team won't work on for several months, stop–you're wasting your time.

Requirements are often one of the most unstable aspects of software development. It's difficult to accurately capture a customer requirement, regardless of the format you use or the amount of effort you put into it. A product backlog with stale items means you wasted time creating requirements that are no longer relevant. Stick with having one to two sprints' worth of "ready" items in the product backlog. Likewise, don't assume that every aspect of a product backlog item needs to be explicitly defined. Allow some room for conversations and creativity about the implementation during a sprint. Ambiguity gives the dev team the opportunity to talk about the best way to complete the PBI and find creative solutions.

Inconsistent PBI Formats

The Scrum Guide doesn't require you to use a specific format for your product backlog, but having a consistent PBI format keeps the backlog organized and makes it easier to interpret.

You'll spend a lot of time working with the product owner and development team to come up with a standard format. You may decide to use different formats for different types of work. (For example, a bug might have an attribute for reproduction steps whereas a new feature might have a value attribute.) Just be sure to use a consistent format for each type of work in your product backlog.

---

1. https://pragprog.com/book/d-jrpredict/predicting-the-unpredictable

Here are some examples of attributes you might decide to require for a new feature:

- Title
- Description
- Acceptance Criteria
- Estimate
- Value

Joe asks:
You keep mentioning estimates, but don't you mean story points?

Story points are just a method for creating estimates. Story points were created by Ron Jeffries to help make estimating easier for Scrum teams. The basic idea behind them is that, instead of estimating a product backlog item in hours, the Scrum team only considers how much effort a PBI will require relative to other PBIs. Teams often use the numbers in the Fibonacci sequence (1, 2, 3, 5, 8, 13) as values for their relative estimates. They'll score work that they think will require less in effort as a 1 or 2, and score more complex work that requires more effort a higher number like an 8 or 13. Teams often use [planning poker](https://en.wikipedia.org/wiki/Planning_poker) to facilitate story-point estimation. The Scrum Guide is silent on how you should estimate work. You can use hours, T-shirt sizes, or story points, or even just mark every product backlog item as a 1 and count how many items you finish in a sprint. Regardless of what technique your team uses, you need to create estimates so the development teams can get a sense of how much work they can pull into a sprint. Remember, estimating is really about the conversations the development team has about their work, and about empowering the product owner to forecast and plan. Exactly how your team creates those estimates is inconsequential.

Here's a product backlog item format that a lot of Scrum teams use—it was created at Connextra[2] in 2001:

"As a (role), I want (behavior), so that I get (business value)."

So what does this format look like in practice? Let's check out an example of a PBI that could end up in a product backlog. But first, some context: Ryan and Todd both teach a lot of Scrum classes, and we need a tool to help us manage our classes. Here's one possible product backlog item that we could decide to order high in our product backlog for this project:

---

2. https://www.agilealliance.org/glossary/user-story-template/

As a Scrum trainer, I want to create a new listing for a Scrum training class so that potential students can get information about the course.

Details: The Scrum trainer needs to be able to enter and edit the following information:

- Course name
- Course description
- Scrum trainer name(s)
- Course location (address)
- Course start date
- Course end date
- A link to register for the course (currently handled through a third-party payment processor)

Value: High - ability to find and register for a course - direct link to revenue
Estimate: Development team estimates five story points for this PBI. The current platform supports the majority of the requested functionality.

As you gather PBIs, your product backlog can start to look like a flat, one-dimensional list that can be challenging to decipher, especially when you consider that the items will be at various level of clarity (story, feature, epic)—in other words, broken down into different levels of detail. To help keep things clear, you can create a list of product backlog items sorted by which level of understanding (decomposition) each PBI is currently in that can be read and understood by the Scrum team and stakeholders.

Epic	Features	Stories
Timesheet	Entry Approval History	Entry - By Employee Entry - By Supervisor Entry - TBD Approval - Employee Submission Approval - Supervisor Rejection Approval - Supervisor Approval History - Of Employee History - Of Supervisor Employees History - TBD
Application Tracking	Submission Candidate Review Interview	Submission - Company Website Submission - LinkedIn Candidate Review - HR Approval Candidate Review - Hiring Manager Approval Candidate Review - Rejection Interview - Scheduling Interview - Feedback
Payroll	TBD	-

Table 2—Sample Levels of Decomposition

What's up with that Payroll item? Great question. In this example, payroll is an epic that's many months away from being considered for a sprint. The Scrum team knows that they need to do the work eventually, but they're not sure what that work looks like yet.

Regardless of the terminology or the format that your team chooses for product backlog items, it's important to be consistent.

The Static Product Backlog

We often see product owners doing everything possible to create the illusion of control and predictability on a project. They create detailed plans and try to fill each and every sprint with PBIs in advance. The PO then creates a Gantt chart to track progress. The product backlog may change ever so slightly so long as the team doesn't deviate too far from the original plan. Incorporating user input is exhausting for the Scrum team and often discouraged by the product owner because the plan has no room for change.

Joe asks:

How many product backlog items does a team need before getting started?

A product-development effort should be backed by a strong vision that guides and informs the Scrum team as they decide what to do next. So long as there are enough product backlog items to bring into the first sprint and formulate a sprint goal, the team should start working. Waste as little time as possible creating a plan for how to start. Be okay with learning as you go and letting the product backlog emerge as you complete your initial PBIs and deliver increments of product.

A static product backlog that doesn't evolve as the team gains experience implies that outcomes are certain—but as anyone who's worked in software knows, outcomes are never certain because circumstances always change. Believing that outcomes are certain traces back to industrial era-type thinking (Taylorism) that we mentioned in Chapter 2, Why Scrum Goes Bad, on page 7. That type of thinking will eventually create tension, angst, and failure. *You can't plan complexity perfectly.* Your goal when starting on a project should be to create a product backlog that contains just enough work to get started with a sprint. The product backlog will grow and change over time as your users and customers provide feedback on the Scrum team's work.

\\// **Joe asks:**
ご゙ # When does the development team look at the product backlog?

The Scrum Guide states that product backlog refinement should consume no more than 10% of a development team's time during a sprint. This guidance helps prevents Scrum teams from looking too far ahead. That said, your Scrum team will look at the product backlog throughout the sprint. If you're using two-week sprints, your team should spend around eight hours doing refinement each sprint.

Scrum was created to facilitate complex, adaptive problem-solving. When you're working on a complex product like developing an embedded control panel or updating a consumer healthcare website, more is unknown than known about what the project will require. It's only by doing the work and getting feedback from your customers that you can know what needs to be built next, and this complexity should be reflected in the product backlog. As the team inspects, adapts, and creates product increments, requirements will emerge. In other words, your teams will learn things and have opportunities to update the product backlog with new information. Don't squander these opportunities in favor of clinging on to false certainty.

Humans like feeling as if the future is certain and we know what tomorrow will bring. Product backlogs often reflects this craving for certainty. Having an exhaustively detailed product backlog that attempts to create certainty feeds this craving but limits the Scrum team's ability to adapt. That will cause the team to build a less valuable product, will limit their creativity, and will set false expectations for stakeholders. Embrace complexity and the lack of certainty that comes with it.

If your PO tries to keep anyone from changing the product backlog, have a chat with them about how it's impossible to predict the future, and how vital it is for the team to be able to adapt to changing conditions. Over the course of our 20-year careers in software and product development, we (your humble authors) have never seen a project hit its estimates perfectly. In every case, adaptation was far more valuable than trying to make perfect predictions.

Your product owner may need some help getting the initial product backlog built or adapting a product backlog that has been static for far too long. In that case, here's a Liberating Structure[3] that can help. It's called 25/10 Crowd

---

3. http://liberatingstructures.com

Sourcing, and it's an idea-generating exercise where the product owner, development team, stakeholders, and users can come together to generate a product backlog.

Invite everyone to a meeting space where there's enough room for people to move around. Then start the exercise:

1. Give each person a blank index card and something to write with.

2. Ask the participants to silently answer the question, "What's the most important feature this product needs to be successful?" Have them write down their answer on one side of the index card. Tell them to hold their cards up in the air when they're done so you can see when everyone is finished.

3. Ask everyone to walk around the room and trade cards—*without reading them.* They should simply mill around the room and exchange cards. Give them 30 seconds or so do to this.

4. Ask each person to rate the idea on their current card from 1 to 5 (with 1 meaning "nope, this isn't an important feature" and 5 meaning "What a wonderful idea. I'm in!") and write that score on the back of the card.

5. Using the same set of cards, repeat steps 3 and 4: Have everyone trade cards and then rate the idea on their current card. Repeat these steps three more times until every card has five scores on the back. At the end of each round, verify the number of scores (which should be the same as the number of completed rounds) by asking each participant to count the number of scores on the back of their current card. At the end of round five, ask the participants to add up the scores on their current card. The result will be a number from 5 to 25.

6. Ask everyone to line up based on the score on their card, and then have the people holding the top ten ideas read their feature out loud, starting with the highest-ranked features.

7. Ask the participants what caught their attention, whether any new ideas for features came to mind during the activity (don't forget to capture these ideas!), and whether they have any input on the highest-ranked items.

Congratulations: you've got a solid foundation for your product backlog! Now it's up to the product owner to adjust the order of features as needed and start refining the highest-ranked PBIs.

And now that your team has a solid product backlog, it's time for the development team to get to work turning those PBIs into high-quality increments.

Today's Forecast: Frustrated Stakeholders

Here's a scenario we've witnessed more than once: During a sprint review, a stakeholder asks when a feature of special interest will be done. The product owner has worked with the development team to be prepared to answer these kinds of questions, and he gives the following answer:

> "Based on what we currently know about the product backlog, the present ordering of product backlog items, and the Scrum team's capacity, that feature will be done six sprints from now."

Eight sprints later, the feature isn't finished. The technical work turned out to be more difficult than the team expected, and new high-priority product backlog items emerged that delayed work on the feature the stakeholder asked about. Regardless, the stakeholder is annoyed and angry about what he views as the empty promise the PO made. Of course, the PO didn't make such a promise—he simply mentioned all the factors that could impact the work—but the stakeholder *interpreted* this as a promise.

Joe asks:

How do I estimate work?

Scrum doesn't require you to estimate work in a specific way. You can use story points, product backlog item counts, or any other variation that you feel is appropriate for your situation. The important thing is that all estimates must come from the people doing the work: the development team.

The stakeholder asked relevant and professional questions. How much longer a feature (or set of features) will take and what the future is going to look like over a specific period of time are questions that a product owner must be able to answer. Exactly *how* the PO answers these questions is incredibly important. A great Scrum master will spend a lot of time coaching the product owner about how to answer stakeholders when the "When will I get my stuff?" question comes up.

Here's an example of how the PO in our scenario could have answered the stakeholder in a clearer, more nuanced way:

> "Given the estimate of that feature and assuming that we don't add any additional product backlog items, we forecast about six sprints. This also assumes that the rest of our estimates are accurate, which we won't know until we complete the work. I would love to sit with you and reevaluate the value proposition of that feature to see how it fits within the roadmap for this product."

This response is better for a number of reasons, some of which are fairly subtle:

- Traditionally, teams were expected to agree and then commit to estimates. Our answer is different: It includes the word "forecast" instead of "commit" to emphasize the lack of certainty.

- It mentions that the product backlog will change.

- It reminds everyone of the unpredictability of the work and the fact that estimates can be wrong.

- The product owner offers to revisit the value proposition of the work, showing that there's flexibility in ordering the product backlog based on value.

Stakeholders want to know how their money is being spent or how they need to pivot their plans to accommodate new feature releases. The development team creates estimates, but the product owner creates and owns the product backlog. The forecasts that a PO uses to answer questions about the release schedule can be provided from two very different perspectives:

- Forecasts based on the release of a feature: when a particular feature will likely be completed.

- Forecasts based on a release date: how many things can likely be delivered by a certain date.

Consider the following high-level product backlog:

Type	Story Point Estimate
Feature A	4
Feature B	5
Defect 1	6
Feature C	2
Feature D	8
Feature E	5
Defect 2	1

Table 3—Sample Product Backlog

Let's imagine a stakeholder wants to know when feature D will be ready—in other words, he wants a forecast based on the delivery of that feature. If the development team has a velocity (that's a fancy way of saying "capacity") of 10 story points per sprint, how many sprints will it take them to deliver feature

A? Using simple math, we know that it will take about three sprints to get that feature delivered as long as the ordering of the PBI's are respected.

How did we get that answer? Feature A and B add up to 9 points, so that's basically one sprint's worth of capacity. (While the team has a velocity of 10 story points per sprint, it's always best to plan on completing *fewer* story points than that in order to give the team a little wiggle room in case any unexpected issues arise.) Defect 1 and feature C add up to 8 points, so there's sprint two. That means feature D will get worked on (and hopefully completed) in sprint three. Of course, when your PO gives this information to the stakeholder, he should add the caveats we discussed earlier.

Now let's pretend that a stakeholder asks how many features in the product backlog can be delivered in six weeks. In that case, the product owner can calculate a forecast based on a release date. Since the development team has a velocity of 10 story points and uses two-week sprints, we can use the same math as above to determine that the team can likely deliver four features in that timeframe: features A, B, C, and D. Again, when the product owner delivers this information to the stakeholder, he should add the caveats we've discussed and really emphasize that, like the weather, this forecast can and will change.

Remind your product owner that you can't estimate complexity perfectly, so he should stop trying. Instead, give stakeholders and customers forecasts based on what you know today, and be transparent by telling them that things can and will change. The ability to forecast and adapt as needed is good! It means you've learned something that can lead to better products.

The Unordered Product Backlog

An unordered product backlog can become a trash heap of PBIs that doesn't give the development team any indication of which items they should work on next. Sprint planning becomes a random grab of what the Scrum team feels is important in that moment. Stakeholders may start lobbying for their pet project, even if those things shouldn't be the team's top priority, and the loudest voice may get precedence.

The product owner determines the order of the product backlog. However, some misguided POs do this by assigning priorities to PBIs, which isn't the same as ordering them, and is an approach that always leads to headaches. For example, Ryan recently worked with a company that was struggling to figure out which product backlog items to work on next. Every PBI in the product backlog was assigned the highest level of priority, 1. What the organization quickly learned is that when everything is important, nothing is important.

Product backlogs should be ordered, not prioritized. The Scrum Guide clearly states that a product backlog is *ordered*—in other words, the product backlog items are in a specific order. The value of each PBI is indicated by where it is ordered on the product backlog.

There are some really good reasons for preferring ordering over prioritization:

- The term "priority" implies a level of certainty that we simply don't have in a complex environment. If your product owner gives a PBI a priority of 1, that implies that the item will get done, and your stakeholders will hear that implicit message loud and clear. And why shouldn't stakeholders assume that PBI will get done—it's of the highest priority!

- If ten PBIs have a priority of 1, how does the development team know which one they should work on first? In short, they don't. But if PBIs are *ordered* instead, the development team knows exactly which ones to work on, and in what order.

- If your product owner has multiple top-priority PBIs, he should know which one delivers the most value to stakeholders—and therefore, he should be able to order the items appropriately. If the PO doesn't know which PBI is most valuable, how can he possibly know whether the sprint should be funded in the first place?

A clearly ordered product backlog creates transparency to stakeholders and helps the dev team know exactly what they should be working on at any given time. So if your product backlog is turning into a trash heap, talk to your product owner about ordering the product backlog items, and offer to help them do so.

Coach's Corner

Sprints are about creating useful increments, not about gathering requirements. Scrum teams should start building the product as soon as possible, not spend their time building their product backlog. But what should they build first? Ordering, as we discussed in the previous section, helps the development team and stakeholders understand which tasks will be performed in what order.

More specifically, the product owner orders the product backlog in a way that maximizes the value of the work that the development team does during the sprint. As a Scrum master, you need to help facilitate this value-centered ordering, especially if your product owner is currently using a priority scheme to sort the product backlog. Here's a liberating structure called Min-Spec[4] that you can use to help your PO identify the most valuable product backlog items. Invite stakeholders, development team members, customers, people in leadership roles in your organization, and others who are interested in the outcome of the product or project.

1. Have the participants form groups of 4-7 people, and provide them with materials for rapidly capturing ideas, tools such as markers and sticky notes, and space to post the ideas (either on a wall or flip chart).

2. Display the current product backlog so that everyone can see it, and then pose this question: "Which features in our product backlog are needed in order to have a successful product release?"

3. Ask each person to write down (one per sticky note) as many must-do product backlog items and must-not-do product backlog items as they can in 2-3 minutes. When time's up, ask the groups to consolidate their individual lists, eliminating duplicates. At this point, each group's list of must-do PBIs will likely be quite large.

4. Have the groups aggressively test all the items on their must-do lists by answering this question about each item: "If we delivered all of our must-do PBIs *except* this one, would we still have a successful product release?" If the answer is "yes," then the group has to delete that PBI from their must-do list. Encourage the teams to be ruthless when answering this question. This step can take around 15-20 minutes, depending on the size of lists. Allow more time as needed.

5. Have the groups compare their work. Ask each group to spend a few minutes sharing their whittled-down, must-do PBI list with everyone, and have them discuss the trade-offs and decisions they made to get to their current list.

6. After each group has presented their lists, have everyone work together to consolidate their lists into one master must-do PBI list that is as short as possible.

7. Have everyone discuss the master list and work together to help the PO order these vital PBIs.

Ryan and Todd work with a lot of product owners who are struggling to order their product backlogs. Sometimes the sheer volume of PBIs makes it difficult

---

4. http://www.liberatingstructures.com/14-min-specs/

for the PO to know where to begin. That's why Min-Spec is such a powerful exercise: The outcome is a list of *essential* product backlog items that will lead to a successful product release. The product owner can use this list to focus on what truly creates value, and order the work in a way that maximizes the development team's efforts.

Speaking of development team, it's time to explore anti-patterns that cause dev teams to struggle. Correcting these bad practices will help you deliver more (and better) product increments, have happier customers, and ensure that your development team is engaged and productive.

CHAPTER 6

The Development Team

Change was in the air at a health insurance company where Todd was consulting, and with it came lots of excitement. The executive team had just approved funding a rewrite of a massive customer portal that was plagued with technical debt. The executives had heard great things about Scrum working well in other companies, and decided to make Scrum the project-management framework for the customer portal rewrite.

A leadership team was put into place that included people with a blend of agile and traditional project management experience. They decided that the following competencies were necessary for success: user experience, front-end development, web-service development, database administration, and infrastructure. They also decided that each competency area would have a product owner—and they hired Todd as one of those POs. (If you've read Chapter 4, The Product Owner, on page 23, you know that having more than one product owner for a product is never a good thing, so this decision didn't bode well for the project.)

Based on these competency areas, the leadership team decided that there should be seven development teams for the project:

Team #	Team Competency
1	Database and Infrastructure
2	Web Services
3	Web Services
4	Front End and User Experience
5	Front End and User Experience
6	Front End and User Experience
7	Front End and User Experience

Table 4—Team Composition

The leadership team quickly hired people with the various skills required for the project, and the development teams got to work. Four months later, the dev teams hadn't delivered a single line of code into any environment, let alone production. Proof of concepts existed for each competency area, but there was no full-stack integration between them. As pressure to deliver mounted, the teams started blaming each other for not fulfilling their obligations.

Nine months after the leadership devised their plan for the teams, the project was canceled. Stakeholders were irate over the amount of money that was spent and the lack of results. As a result of the project being an utter failure, 60 people lost their jobs.

There were many factors that led to this disaster, and in this chapter we'll suggest ways to avoid similar issues on your projects. We'll discuss various anti-patterns illustrated by this story, as well as other common ones we've encountered. Some of the issues we'll describe are caused by poor decision-making that's outside the development team's control, while others are things the team *can* control. As a Scrum master, you need to be able to tackle both types of scenarios. We'll teach you techniques that can help ensure your development teams succeed.

Lacking Necessary Skills

Scrum doesn't prescribe how development teams should be constructed. It simply requires that teams deliver a done increment of software at the end of every sprint. (See Chapter 13, Deconstructing the Done Product Increment, on page 163 for more about what "done" means.) So how *should* you construct development teams?

In the scenario we just described, the teams were organized by area of expertise. (These are called competency-based teams or component teams.) This way of arranging things fits into traditional organizational management structures, so it's common for companies that are new to Scrum to organize their dev teams this way. In waterfall projects, for example, these competency areas are phase gates: Competency teams hand off their part of the project after their phase is complete. Here is a common example of waterfall project gates:

1. Analysis
2. Design
3. Development
4. Testing
5. Deployment

The five gates happen sequentially. For instance, when analysis finishes, design begins—there's no going back.

But competency-based teams don't typically work in Scrum because it means that each team depends on other teams to make progress. Why is that a problem? Because in Scrum, a development team needs to have all the skills necessary to create a done increment every sprint—without relying on anyone outside the team. In the health insurance scenario at the beginning of this chapter, the teams got stuck because they had to depend on each other for things they couldn't do themselves, which brought the whole project to a standstill.

When deciding how to construct a development team, it's vital to think about what "done" means for your project. "Done", as prescribed by Scrum, means that each increment is potentially releasable into production—there's no work left to be completed before the increment can be shipped. This includes analysis, design, development, and testing. You can think of a sprint as a mini-project where all of these traditional activities occur. A development team needs to have every necessary competency in order to make that a reality. This is commonly referred to as a *cross-functional* team. Cross-functional teams can make swift progress and create done increments every sprint because they're self-sufficient—they don't have to depend on anyone else to make progress.

> ## Joe asks:
> ## Who determines development team composition?
>
> Deciding the team composition should be a collective effort lead by the product owner. The product owner owns the vision for a project but may not know what skills are needed to bring that vision to fruition. The PO should enlist the help of management, the Scrum master, and relevant technical experts to determine what skills the team needs to turn that vision into a product.
>
> Once development is under way, the development team should regularly assess whether they do in fact have all the skills they need to be truly cross-functional and independent. If they do not, they need to acknowledge this ASAP and enlist help from other members of the Scrum team and the organization to find folks that can fill the skill gaps.

Several months into the health insurance project that we described at the beginning of this chapter, Todd alerted the executive team that, if they wanted the project to have any chance of success, they desperately needed to create cross-functional teams with all the skills necessary for getting to done. As a last ditch effort to save the project, the executives took his advice. Unfortunately, it was too little, too late, and the project still failed. But it was interesting to witness *how* the teams became cross-functional and what happened after they did.

Once the executives decided to reorganize the teams, they held a meeting that included everyone involved in the project, and announced their decision. They explained that each new team needed to be able to *independently* output a done increment at the end of every sprint. The executives then asked the existing teams to self-organize into new, cross-functional teams. (The executives were skeptical of this self-selecting approach—which Todd had suggested—but they were desperate and agreed to give it a shot.) The result of this exercise was eight development teams that each had all the skills needed to meet the new demands.

The impact of this change was incredible. Before the reorg, the area where the development teams sat was quiet and filled with tension, and sprint reviews involved blame and angst. After the reorg, the team area was buzzing with excitement and collaboration, and sprint reviews became productive, collaborative working sessions: Members discussed the product vision, usage, and outlook, as well as quality concerns, and impediments they faced. Leadership and the Scrum teams were actually talking and starting to work together. Stakeholders were floored at the progress the new teams made during their first sprint. The teams were turning product backlog items that were in their sprint backlogs into done increments. They could own a problem and deliver a solution from end to end—and that's exactly what they did. The reorganization created major momentum to move the project forward.

Sadly, behind the scenes, executives had already made the decision to cut the project budget before the new teams formed. However, the improvement in what was happening on the project after the reorganization was abundantly clear. The teams worked in their new cross-functional capacity for five sprints with astonishing results. This made the final decision to defund the project very hard for stakeholders, but they went ahead with it anyway. Imagine what might have happened had the teams been cross-functional from the start!

When a development team has all the skills necessary to solve a problem without needing help from anyone outside of the team, they have the ability to collaborate around the problem and find a solution—in other words, to truly self-organize. If they lack important skills, they'll get stuck, frustration will build, undone work will accumulate, and your project may very well fail.

A quick and effective way to determine whether your team needs additional skillsets is to map out the flow of work required to get a product backlog item from inception to production. For example, for a team Todd recently worked with, the flow looked like this:

1. Analysis/Refinement
2. Wireframes
3. Coding
4. Testing
5. Deployment

If you identify an area that requires skills or people outside of the development team, then you've found an impediment to tackle. In Todd's case, he discovered that the deployment workflow required the development team to rely on outside people to get software into production. They resolved this impediment by implementing additional deployment automation and by getting someone from the infrastructure team to join the development team.

That's Not My Job

A development team can have all the skills necessary to solve a problem, but not take advantage of them. Just like it's possible to have whole development teams that are siloed by area of expertise, similar silos can exist *within* a development team, too. As a result, team members may refuse to reach outside the bounds of their competency to get an increment to done.

For example, let's say there are two days left in a sprint. The dev team is done coding, but they still need to do a full regression test on a website to consider the work done. In the daily scrum, the tester comments that he doesn't think he'll have the time to finish and asks if anyone is willing to help. A software engineer responds, "I'm a Java developer—I shouldn't have to execute test scripts. Can you develop in Java if I'm behind?"

This kind of comment is quite harsh but, unfortunately, isn't uncommon, especially in companies that have switched from waterfall project management to Scrum. In waterfall, competencies are phases: When coding is done, the coding phase is marked as complete and coders move on to the next thing. Their accountability stops at writing code.

You can sometimes also trace the root cause of this type of mentality to the organization's reporting structure. It's common to have testers report to a test manager, engineers report to an engineering manager, designers report to a design manager, and so on. The bounds of accountability stop at the manager for that particular vertical. This can create an "us versus them" mentality, which may have existed in the organization for quite some time.

In Scrum, there's only one title on a development team: developer. A developer on a Scrum team might write code, develop test cases, create user interface designs, write customer documentation, and so on. Regardless of an individual team member's area of expertise, the whole team has a single accountability: to deliver an increment at the end of the sprint. If the design is complete but coders can't finish their work by the end of the sprint, that's the *whole team's* problem to fix.

Is this anti-pattern happening on your team? If so, use your next retrospective to create shared accountability of the increment. Map out all the hands a product backlog item must touch before it's considered done. Often this will result in a flow across the different competencies on the team (for example: to-do, analysis, design, development, testing, and done). After you've defined this flow, start asking questions:

- Is any part of this flow more accountable for the increment than any other?

- If a product backlog item gets stuck, is there anything anybody outside of that competency can do to help to move it forward?

- If a product backlog item doesn't meet the definition of done by the end of the sprint, whose fault is it?

- If this team fails, are some roles more accountable for the failure than others?

- What can we do, starting next sprint, to collectively own the outcome of the sprint?

Creating whole-team ownership can be challenging. Try taking a coaching stance and asking questions that foster conversations between team members. The reality is that no one role within the team is the hero. A development team succeeds or fails together, and it's up to us as Scrum masters to create awareness of that.

Cutting Corners

Imagine a development team that seems to be moving at the speed of light. No matter how many items are brought into a sprint, they always appear to be accomplished at the end. But as the months pass, that speed exponentially slows down. Production bugs continually interrupt the sprint backlog, often making the sprint goal unachievable, and stakeholders are surprised by the lack of progress after such a fast start and how hard the team is working.

During a sprint retrospective, the development team had a heart to heart. They admitted that their early success was due to some short-sighted architectural decisions that were supposed to be temporary, and that they had been ignoring their definition of done for the past few months. The development team wanted to maintain the pace they had set to please the customers and stakeholders who were counting on them. The temporary decisions became permanent and, to keep things moving, the team intentionally ignored their definition of done. As they built more on top of the platform, it got harder and harder to add new functionality. The copy-and-paste method the team had been using was no longer working. They had created a large amount of technical debt.

Joe asks:

How often should a team finish all the items in their sprint backlog?

In the old-school waterfall mentality, success is defined as being on scope, on time, and within the budget. When organizations adopt to Scrum, these waterfall definitions of success often carry over, which can be problematic because Scrum defines success differently. In Scrum, we take a product mentality where success is defined by delighting our customers with high-quality, valuable products. We do this by creating done product increments that are potentially shippable every sprint. This gives the product owner the option to incrementally ship product so they can frequently get customer feedback on what the dev team has built.

In [xxx](#chapter.sprintplanning), we discuss the importance of having a sprint goal. By focusing on accomplishing this goal and not on trying to finish all the product backlog items, we target a business-value based outcome (an increment of product that could bring value to a stakeholder). Trying to finish all the PBIs in the sprint backlog is waterfall thinking. In Scrum, it doesn't matter how many PBIs the development team finishes each sprint so long as they've met the sprint goal.

When a project starts, it's impossible to know exactly what kind of architectural patterns and practices will be best for the end product. Architecture should be a constant concern of the development team, and something that they regularly discuss throughout each sprint. The best architectures emerge in the same way the product backlog does, and should be validated by the development team as the product is built and delivered to customers.

A key component of developing an architecture that's fit for purpose—meaning it meets the organization's and customer's current needs (and their likely future ones)—is a team's definition of done. As we discuss in detail in Chapter 13, Deconstructing the Done Product Increment, on page 163, the Scrum team creates this definition, providing a clear understanding within the team of what it means for something to be considered done. It also creates transparency with the product owner so that, when the development team says they are done, the PO knows exactly what that means.

Be sure to read Chapter 13, Deconstructing the Done Product Increment, on page 163 for more about defining done, but for now here's a quick rundown. A development team's definition of done should evolve over time, becoming more strict as a team matures. Evaluating and changing it should be part of every sprint retrospective. For example, a team's initial definition of done might be something like this:

• Code has been reviewed by someone other than the person who wrote it.
• The PBI has been tested by someone other than the person who developed it.
• The PBI has been deployed to the development environment.
• The PBI has been tested by someone besides the code reviewer or the person who wrote it.

Many sprints later, this team's definition of done might evolve into this:

• Automated tests have been written.
• The code passes the continuous integration build.
• The functionality is sitting in the staging environment ready for deployment.

The difference in these two definitions is substantial. A lot of architectural considerations, practices, and organizational constraints need to be resolved to get from the first definition to the second. This maturation shows that the team isn't cutting corners but is instead trying to advance their capabilities to get to a releasable increment—which is required by Scrum.

What if a development team has a definition of done that they continually revise but which they don't actually *abide* by? This will cause decreased transparency across the entire Scrum team, undone work, low-quality work, and the degradation of the Scrum values. It's a scary situation that we've seen happen, and it comes with dire consequences.

Cutting corners by ignoring the definition of done trades short-term gains for long-term losses. These long-term losses can scar an organization and may put your product in an unrecoverable state. Even worse, ignoring the definition of done can cause irreparable damage to your company's reputation. A development team must create a solution that is fit for the purpose but also considers a holistic design that can encompass the future of the product and the organization.

What can your team do to evaluate and evolve its definition of done? Examine your existing definition and think about the next things to add to it, and what the team hopes it will look like in the future. To get started, draw the diagram as shown on page 66, on a whiteboard or flip chart. Then have the development team place sticky notes in each of the three sections:

- Now: Our definition of done as it stands today. What are we capable of right now? For instance, in our earlier example, this section would contain the following:

  - Code has been reviewed by someone other than the person who wrote it.

  - The PBI has been tested by someone other than the person who developed it.

  - The PBI has been deployed to the development environment.

  - The PBI has been tested by someone besides the code reviewer or the person who wrote it.

- Next: What do we plan to do next to advance our architectural practices and make our definition of done more strict? Again, pulling from the earlier example:

  - Automated tests have been written.

  - The code passes the continuous integration build.

  - The functionality is sitting in the staging environment, ready for deployment.

- Future: What things do we imagine being in our definition of done once we're capable of them in the future? Here are some possibilities for our example scenario:

  - The PBI passes all automated tests (unit, integration, and functional).

  - The PBI has been reviewed by the entire Scrum team.

  - The PBI has been shipped into production.

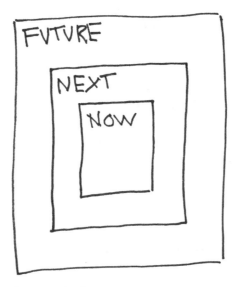

Revisit this exercise frequently during sprint retrospectives to help evolve the team's definition of done.

Everyone for Themselves

Todd worked with a Scrum team where, at the end of sprint planning, development team members would choose and self-assign which product backlog items they were accountable for accomplishing during a sprint. The team members would then go back to their desks and each person would focus just on *their* PBIs, and had little interaction with other team members.

The team's daily scrum conversations centered around individual developers updating other development team members on what progress they'd made on their PBIs, while other team members barely listened while awaiting their turns. Many sprints passed without the team completing their sprint goal. On the team's Scrum board, almost everything sat in the in-progress category during each sprint.

Alas, we see this situation quite often: development team members leaving the sprint planning meeting and working on PBIs in isolation throughout the sprint. One of the biggest causes of this anti-pattern is that many organizations still operate under the illusion that they must maximize resource utilization, and that more is accomplished when individuals work on different items than when they collaborate. (We've heard many developers argue this—it's not just management.) But just because there's a lot of work in progress doesn't mean there will be a lot of work finished at the end of a sprint. That's because a development team can't self-organize around a problem if team members don't work together. And if every team member is working on something different, then ownership over the increment (a key component of Scrum) turns into ownership of individual product backlog items.

Reducing the number of product backlog items that are in progress may be the just recipe you need to create better focus and help your team get a high-quality, done increment at the end of the sprint. If your team is plagued by too much work in progress, during your next retrospective, try suggesting that you experiment with a WIP (work in progress) limit. Take these steps:

1. Define when a PBI becomes "active" in a sprint—in other words, when work has officially started taking place on it. This active state could progress through a workflow, such as analysis, design, coding, and testing. All of those states in this example are considered "active."

2. Next, define when work is considered "done" in a sprint—when the PBI is releasable.

3. Limit the number of items that can be active at any given time. Have the team choose a reasonable number to limit themselves to. Start high, as you can always decrease this number.

4. In the next sprint retrospective, review the effect of instituting this limit.

Limiting work in progress is one technique you can suggest to foster collaboration. There are many other techniques that you may suggest such as pair programming, code reviews, or mob programming. The goal is to get a team truly working as a *team* and not as a bunch of individuals, each trying to complete their own work. The team will have a far greater chance of creating a high-quality product if they collaborate.

Wait Your Turn

A few years ago, Todd worked with a development team as a Scrum master. The product we were working on was a slick engineering sales tool which was well-liked and well-received by the users. The development team took pride in the quality of their work, the team's chemistry was great, and everyone genuinely liked working together.

During one sprint retrospective, a mechanical engineer on the team was quiet and looked exhausted, and others noticed that he wasn't acting like himself. After some prodding by the team, he opened up about what was bothering him:

> Every single sprint, you guys race out of the gate, taking on the things that take you a while to develop. I, in contrast, sit for the first few days with hardly anything to do. Toward the end of every sprint, when you all are winding down, I'm winding up and working 16-hour days to test the results of what you've developed. It's completely exhausting.

The software engineers realized he was right. Their opinions completely dominated sprint planning. And when they created a plan for the next 24 hours during the daily scrum, the mechanical engineer was rarely considered. This wasn't deliberate or malicious—it just happened.

During every sprint, teams should find ways to nonsequentially execute work. A sprint *shouldn't* be a mini-waterfall project where each area of expertise has to wait for their turn, like this:

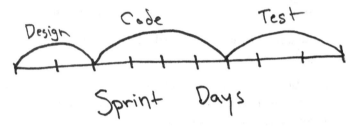

See how coding has to wait for design to finish and testing has to wait for coding to finish? This will cause a lot of grief as the team rushes to finish an increment by the end of every sprint. (We used design, coding, and testing in this example, but your situation may include things like analysis, infrastructure, deployment, and so on.)

Ideally, development teams should be able to nonsequentially execute work, like so:

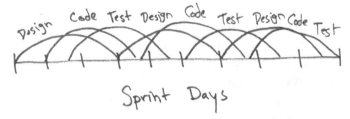

Nonsequential execution allows the team members to work together as single unit, always considering each other. A single area of expertise doesn't "own" the plan for the sprint or the day—instead, they are owned by the entire development team and everybody's input is incorporated. This requires thoughtfulness and consideration, especially for teams that aren't used to working together.

The solution that Todd's team (in the example) came up with was brilliant. They decided that the best way to be cognizant of this issue was to further visualize their sprint backlog. They created a "wall of testing" specifically to enhance transparency around the flow of work to the mechanical engineer. The idea was that the visualization would build awareness around the nonsequential execution of work that was necessary to build a good product. They came up with the analogy that the mechanical engineer should be constantly fed like Pac Man. The analogy and the visual board worked great for this team.

The Team Is Too Big

Two years ago, Todd was an Agile coach helping a new Scrum master, Jessica, get acclimated to her new role. The first chance they had to jointly observe the development team was when they attended the daily scrum by phone with a few team members in the room. As the meeting time approached, they were both struck by the number of "dings" signaling more people joining the call. In total, 29 people attended.

The development team had grown from 10 to 29 people over the previous year and a half. More people were added as the team became overwhelmed by the numerous projects they were tasked with. In the eyes of management, it was easier to manage a single team than multiple teams, and the team seemed to be doing fine, so there was no urgency to change the team dynamic by splitting them up.

As Todd and Jessica observed the meeting, dysfunctions in the team started to show. There were all kinds of personality types: heroes, firefighters, drifters, you name it. Heck, one person barely showed up to work at all. The team had no concept of incremental delivery nor did they have anything resembling a sprint backlog. They simply had a daily task list that was the discussion point for their 45-minute daily scrums.

Have you ever participated in a daily scrum with 29 people? It's an overwhelming experience. The purpose of the event gets lost with that many people involved. So, how many people *should* be on a development team?

The Scrum Guide recommends that a dev team consist of between three and nine people, but that isn't a hard and fast rule. However, we recommend that you stick to that 3-9 recommendation because experience has shown us that communication starts to degrade if there are more than nine people on the development team. There are, of course, exceptions to this as the team needs to have all the skills to deliver a done increment, but these exceptions are rare.

We've talked quite a lot about development team accountability in this chapter. Can a team that exceeds the recommended nine-person size limit effectively self-organize around a problem and have collective ownership of a done increment? Perhaps, but it takes a lot of effort.

There aren't many sports that have 29-person teams. It would be awfully hard to keep everyone coordinated, plus there's no way everyone on the field could effectively communicate with each other. If this is true of sports, think how much worse it is in a complex profession like software development.

Is a large team a problem in your organization? Rather than *you* trying to decide on a new team construction, ask the team to self-organize into new teams. To get started, gather everyone into a large room. Next and most important, make sure everyone understands that the new teams should be no larger than nine people and that each team should have all the skills needed to deliver a done increment of work by the end of each sprint. You can add a fun twist and ask each team to give itself a funny name such as a superhero power or video game. Finally, set a time limit for this activity so there's an urgency for the group to arrive at a solution fairly quickly. Depending on the number of people, two hours is probably sufficient, though you might need to increase that limit for larger groups.

Letting a team organize themselves into smaller teams may sound like a leap of faith, but it's something that we've done several times with a lot of success. By giving teams the autonomy to do this reorganizing, they immediately start thinking of themselves more as a team rather than a collection of individuals. And if, down the road, you find that the teams need to be reorganized again, you can simply repeat this process.

Not Taking the Initiative

Scrum Master: *Is everybody busy enough today?*

Developer: *I'm waiting on some feedback from the tester before I do anything else.*

Scrum Master: *Grab another item from the sprint backlog and start working on it. We all have to stay busy.*

If this conversation sounds familiar, you're not alone: Todd has done this too and he's not proud of it. It's a trap that can happen in any sprint when we, as Scrum masters, view ourselves as task masters whose job is to keep everybody busy. This often results from outside pressures—frequently from management trying to make sure everyone is working at maximum capacity. It's common for management to think that sprints are about getting as much work done as possible, and that the most effective way to do that is to keep everyone as busy as possible. But as you know, the outcome of a sprint isn't about that: It's about the development team creating a done and potentially shippable product increment.

So what *should* a designer do if they finish their work halfway through a sprint? What should coders do while testers are validating that everything works, especially toward the end of a sprint? And what should testers do at the beginning of a sprint?

Scrum doesn't recognize specializations in title. Everyone on a development team has the same title: developer. That's not to say that various members of the dev team don't have specialized skills—they will and should. But they should always be willing to pitch in to help achieve the sprint goal, even if it requires doing things that aren't in their areas of expertise. Not doing so can cause all kinds of headaches. For example, if the coders are getting ahead of the testers every sprint, eventually the coders will be a full sprint ahead and the testers will be a full sprint behind. If coders try to start work for an upcoming sprint instead of lending a hand with testing, they risk creating waste. The team can't predict the future, and technically the next sprint hasn't been planned, plus they don't have feedback on the current increment. Because we don't know what the customer wants, there's no way to "get ahead," so trying to do so just wastes time and effort.

As we've said, collaboration is critical to a development team's success, and lending a hand wherever necessary is a great way to foster collaboration. If a development team doesn't collaborate, they run the risk of excluding experts from different domains when decisions are being made about the product. For example, if designers work in a box, not sharing the reasoning behind their design, the architecture might not be capable of supporting their design. And if coders "work ahead" while the testers work on their growing list of tasks, then testers aren't part of the decision-making process. Perhaps they're even being excluded from estimation, which means the team misses out on their valuable insights into ways the team could perform the work.

As we discussed in the "Everyone for Themselves" section earlier in this chapter, limiting the amount of work in progress and having conversations about managing the flow of work can help to bring these bottlenecks to light during a sprint. It's important that all domain experts on a team work hand-in-hand. Could one area of expertise hand off pieces of work earlier to another one? And can the team coordinate the handoffs to make them smaller and create less of a backlog? Or better yet, can they work together simultaneously on something? Often the answer is "yes."

Even if the development team has minimized the handoffs, made work as collaborative as possible, and fully integrated their work with systems and other teams, at the end of the sprint—whether that's the last two days or the last week—everyone on the team can and should help with any work that needs to get done to achieve the sprint goal.

While no one should do work for the sake of looking busy, there's always work that team members can do, even if it's not the type of work they normally specialize in. The whole development team is accountable for the increment at the end of the sprint. No one person gets the credit for success or the blame for failure—we succeed or fail together.

Coach's Corner

The development team is accountable for delivering high-quality increments of potentially shippable product every sprint. Nobody can tell them how to accomplish this work and they must have all the skills necessary to make that happen. There are no sub-roles on the development team because no role dominates any other. Collaboration is the fabric of a successful development team. They achieve the sprint goal and genuinely care about the quality of the product and of the underpinning architecture.

As a Scrum master, it's extremely important to remember that the development team has ownership of their work—not you. It's easy for Scrum masters to forget that they're servant leaders, not taskmasters. If you find yourself dictating what your development team should do, step back and read Chapter 7, Embracing the Scrum Master Role, on page 75 for a reminder of what your role *should* be. It's unhealthy and counterproductive for a development team to lack ownership over their process.

To help give the development team more accountability over their process, try this exercise during your next sprint retrospective:

1. Gather the development team together. Ask each person to silently spend one minute brainstorming as many team improvements as they can think of (process, technical, and so on), and to write each idea on a separate sticky note. To get them inspired, try offering a phrase for them to complete, such as "In order for us to become a rock-star development team, we have to..."

2. After the one minute is up, ask them to pair up with another person and spend two minutes collaborating and writing down yet more improvement ideas together.

3. After these two minutes are up, have the pairs share an idea one at a time by shouting it out and placing it on a whiteboard.

4. Ask the group to look for patterns, and if any emerge, group the related sticky notes together. Discuss all the topics for five minutes, paying specific attention to the patterns.

5. Lastly, give each person three sticker dots. Tell them to put the dots on what they think are the most pressing items. They can place all three dots on the same sticky note or distribute them across various sticky notes.

Catalog the results and make them visible in the team area. Use the dots to help prioritize: Address the items with the most dots first. Choose one or two of these improvements to implement in the next sprint, and then revisit the list during the next sprint retrospective. Look carefully at the list for signs of impediments, and if there's something going on that the development team can't resolve on their own, be sure to take action.

You've just seen one of the many ways in which you can help ensure your development team succeeds. In the next chapter, we'll dive into how you can truly embrace the Scrum master role and empower your team.

CHAPTER 7

Embracing the Scrum Master Role

A passive Scrum master is one consistent factor of a failed sprint. Ryan once had this conversation:

Scrum Master: *I'm having trouble staying busy. I go to the daily scrum and help facilitate it. I also plan out the refinement meetings and prepare retrospective formats, but toward the end of the week, I really don't have much to do. I'm honestly kind of bored.*

Ryan: *Interesting. Has the team delivered any features yet?*

Scrum Master: *No. They're having trouble with code merges and integration testing. It's been three sprints since we've been able to get to production.*

Ryan: *Are the team members getting along? How are the retrospectives going?*

Scrum Master: *Actually, there are a few personality conflicts that really bog down the team with drama. The last retrospective was a total dumpster fire. The team can't seem to agree on what to do next. One of the developers stormed out midway through and we haven't seen another all week.*

Ryan: *Seems like you have plenty to do! Let's capture a few ideas and see if we can put a plan together to help your team get back on track.*

The Scrum master role requires continual introspection as you navigate the choppy waters of organizational, individual, and team dynamics. When you, the Scrum Master, lose sight of your responsibility to act as a servant leader, that's when bad Scrum can happen.

The Scrum master's role is to:

- Make sure the team and organization understand and enact Scrum by applying the Scrum principles and practices to interactions between the team members, stakeholders, and others in the organization.

- Facilitate Scrum events as needed to help everyone adhere to the Scrum roles and rules.

> ### Joe asks:
> ## What does it mean to be a servant leader?
>
> The servant-leader philosophy means that, above all else, service to others is the most important aspect of leadership. A servant leader puts others' needs first. The primary interest of a servant leader is to enable and support others to grow and prosper because that's the best way to foster both individual and team success. This is in stark contrast to traditional leadership, where accumulating power and authority are the primary concerns.

- Infuse life into the Scrum framework by coaching team members on how to embrace and live the Scrum values.

- Act as servant leader for the team, *not* as the team boss.

- Lead with influence and empathy while focusing on the needs of the Scrum team members and the customers they serve.

- Spark change that aims to improve product quality and project outcomes.

- Embody the Scrum values to the organization.

Your goal as Scrum master is to help the team maximize value, reduce risk, and deliver outcomes that align to the organization's product vision through the effective use of Scrum. The Scrum master role is both rewarding and a full-time commitment. It's a difficult job for which Ryan and Todd have made many mistakes. We're writing this book so that you can learn from our failures and successes as Scrum masters.

Let's explore the common anti-patterns of the Scrum master role. A Scrum master should have a low tolerance for impediments. Many of these anti-patterns happen when that's not the case. Don't be that Scrum master. If the anti-patterns we describe in this chapter are present on your team, it's time to jump into action and resolve them quickly. Otherwise, you're an impediment to your Scrum team's success.

No One on My Team Knows Scrum

A Scrum master is a teacher. Part of the role is to ensure that Scrum is well-understood and enacted by the Scrum team. Want a quick way to test whether your teaching efforts have been successful? At the end of your next daily scrum, ask the dev team if they can draw the Scrum framework on a whiteboard and explain the Scrum roles, artifacts, and events.

Joe asks:
What's the difference between a Scrum master and an Agile coach?

About $50 per hour.

Seriously though, there isn't a hierarchy that starts at Scrum Master and ends at Enterprise Agile Coach. The difference between the two roles comes down to where the work is focused. An Agile coach is focused on the organization and then works inward to teams and individuals. The Scrum master is focused on the Scrum team and works outward toward the organization. While it's possible—and part of the role —for a Scrum master to act as an Agile coach to the organization, not all Agile coaches have the skills and knowledge to act as a Scrum master. In fact, in organizations where the Scrum master is fully empowered to fulfill their role, Agile coaches are often unnecessary.

If that seems like a big ask, try something simpler. Ask your team who has read the latest version of The Scrum Guide. Over the past five years, we've yet to find a team where every team member can answer "yes" the first time we ask that question. We ourselves might have answered "no" to this question many years ago, when we were development team members.

When you teach Scrum, you need the skills to present the Scrum framework in a compelling and engaging way. Do you have tools and techniques that allow your students to participate actively in the learning? We encourage you to use every drawing in this book with your teams to teach the Scrum framework in an interactive way.

Remember the Scrum diagram we showed you in Chapter 1? It's great for visualizing Scrum. But sometimes it can be helpful to do team exercises with an *unlabeled* version of that diagram, like this:

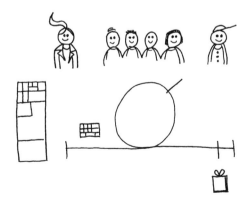

For example, try writing the Scrum roles, events, and artifacts on a single color of sticky notes. Ask your team to place any sticky note they choose on the diagram and discuss an important fact about the item they put on the board. Once the first person has shared their fact, elaborate further on the selected sticky note and provide additional insights and context. As team members place more notes on the board, discuss how those roles, events, and artifacts are related.

Don't immediately correct wrong answers. In fact, don't touch a single sticky note during the entire exercise. Hold the space. See if someone else will help out. If the team needs a cue, ask if something might be out of place.

This exercise helps your team get its first taste of self-organization and team learning. Don't take that away from them. You could very easily spend two to three hours on this exercise. If that seems like too long for one meeting, break it up into half-hour sessions each day until all the stickies are in the right spots. You'll be amazed at the insights you gain each time you run this exercise with your teams and the organization.

It's not uncommon for people to misunderstand Scrum but be too afraid to ask for clarification–that's why exercises like the one we just described are so valuable. It's important that team members have a shared understanding of the Scrum framework, principles and values. Interpretations will change over time so it's a good idea to run through this exercise every few months.

Help! I'm the Impediment

As a new Scrum master, you'll likely struggle with a hard truth about the role: It's not about you.

Your focus as a Scrum master is on helping the Scrum team successfully deliver valuable software by the end of each sprint. Your commitment is to put the needs of your team and the organization ahead of your own needs, wants, and agendas.

Not everyone is meant to be a Scrum master. If you understand Scrum well, you can perform the role. But the gap between a Scrum master fixated on only the mechanics of Scrum, and a Scrum master who lives the Scrum values, favors self-organization, and leads with a servant's heart, is vast and wide.

If you're transitioning to the Scrum master role from a project management background, this transition will be difficult. There will be times when self-organization doesn't feel right or make sense. You'll have a tendency to put the focus back on yourself and to show how you've solved problems.

You may try to increase velocity, thinking that speed is what you're after, rather than delivering value sooner. You'll be tempted to assign tasks because you may believe that you know who should do the work better than the development team does. These behaviors may have served you well in the past, but in the context of Scrum, they're impediments that need to be removed.

Speaking of impediments, it's tempting for a Scrum master to want to resolve every single impediment that the team faces. But it's far more effective to stay out of the development team's way. Instead, help them find ways to remove the impediments themselves. This preserves self-organization and promotes empowerment and whole-team accountability.

I Was an Impediment

by: Ryan Ripley

Confession time: Early in my career, a project manager asked me to join her for lunch. We sat down and discussed some questions she had about Scrum. At the time, I was the only Scrum master at the company. She needed help. She asked about hybrid models—if Scrum and waterfall could coexist. Rather than using these questions as an opportunity to understand her worries and fears about the move to Scrum, I went on a rant against waterfall. Why would anyone want to keep that practice when it led to past failures? She smiled, finished her lunch, and left.

Later on, I realized that she wasn't defending waterfall. She was terrified of moving to Scrum and she was looking for ways to make the hybrid work. She wanted to see herself in this new future, and I didn't help her. I made the change even more scary. I blew an opportunity to bring an ally on board as we adopted Scrum.

The surest way to avoid these bad Scrum patterns is to ask the team, "Am I enabling, empowering, and serving you?" This is a great sprint retrospective activity, especially if you have concerns that you've become an impediment to your team.

A word of warning: Sometimes you won't know whether you're helping or impeding the team. The Scrum master role has many stances, activities, and options. Some actions might be helpful in one stage of team maturity, but harmful in another. So can you know which is which? Ask your team and keep yourself rooted to empiricism.

When you take an action, do you know the outcome you're after? If not, don't act. Think a bit and then try something else. Avoid the trap of acting impulsively without a clear goal in mind by staying laser-focused on serving your teams and helping them find ways to deliver products.

Daily journaling is also helpful. Write down notes about interactions you have and events that happen throughout the day: What went well? What did you struggle with? What weren't you sure about? As you think about each entry,

try to remember whether you were giving direction or whether you were asking questions.

Looking at your ratio of statements to questions can lead to insights into how you're doing. Take each entry and try to apply the Scrum values to the people, events, or situations. Are you modeling behavior that embodies the Scrum values? Are you favoring self-organization?

You ask the Scrum team to inspect and adapt their work. Why should it be any different for you? Generate insights from your journaling and find creative experiments to try next.

An experiment you might try is to spend a day trying to reply only with questions during conversations with the team. See if you can refrain from solving problems directly and instead reveal solutions by asking leading questions that let the individuals and the team come to their own conclusions. If an entire day seems too monumental, then try an hour. Asking powerful questions is an art form that requires practice.

Give it a try. You may learn something about yourself and your teams.

The Superhero Scrum Master

Scrum teams work on complex problems. Solutions emerge iteratively and incrementally. If you try to become a "hero" by mandating solutions, you can cause lasting damage to the team. We both know this "hero" position all too well, unfortunately. It's a tempting stance that both of us have taken in the past—and then we had to unwind a lot of bad behavior that we'd caused.

The Superhero Scrum Master is addicted to the adrenaline rush, praise, and attention that comes from solving problems. Their work isn't about the team. It's about increasing their status or their visibility, showing how they've contributed, and being the hero. Here's what Superhero Scrum Master Ryan or Todd might have sounded like in the past:

"I'd prefer to be considered someone who helped the team get past the hurdles and obstacles and dragged them across the finish line. We can have a laugh later about how silly the development team's behavior was during the sprint. For now, I got them to deliver."

These aren't exactly the words of someone who believes in preserving self-organization and favoring a whole-team mentality. But when we exhibited this behavior, we truly believed that we were acting in the best interest of the team. As we've learned, there are consequences to this mentality:

- No ability to experiment: When a Scrum master "solves" all the team's problems, the team won't learn how to experiment. A Scrum master must constantly inspect and adapt practices. Some changes work—others don't. Dictating answers robs the team of these lessons.

- Scrum team members withdraw: Apathy sets in when a Scrum master mandates solutions. A disengaged team can lead to silos of knowledge and individual actors instead of a gelled and cohesive Scrum team.

- Whole-team concept is compromised: Every member of the Scrum team contributes to the product and code base. If a hero Scrum Master is solving all the problems, the Scrum team becomes dependent on this hero behavior. Coaching others to solve issues and impediments can help teams grow, mature, and find success together.

The superhero mentality is often the result of old-style leadership practices taking hold in an organization:

- Carrot-and-Stick Mentality: "Failure isn't an option. Why would I let a team go down a path that I *know* is wrong? Seems like I could be blamed if I could have stopped the issue before it happened." Experiments and learning aren't valued in a blame-centric culture.

- Bad Scrum: In many cases, the team isn't following Scrum, and without the heroic Scrum master, essential activities would get lost. The Scrum master needs to manage these activities because nobody else will do it. But when a Scrum master decides that he or she knows best and starts dictating solutions to problems that may or may not be actual problems, they're robbing the team of learning opportunities, improvements, and earned lessons.

Scrum master heroics can appear to help in the short term, but over time, the negative impacts are amplified.

The sprint retrospective can help unmask a Superhero Scrum Master. If your team has raised concerns about you, the Scrum master, making decisions for them, take the opportunity to facilitate a retrospective around who made the decisions during a sprint. If you find yourself in a situation where you think you might be the hero, have the courage to ask. Todd did this during a retrospective after noticing some eye rolls from the team during a sprint review. He was floored to find out he was unintentionally being the hero:

> *Todd:*   *Am I overbearing or quick to make a decision for the team?*
>
> *Brave Team Member:*   *Well, you do drive every conversation with stakeholders during the sprint review and don't really let us talk. So yes, you do.*
>
> *Todd:*   *Gulp...*

You can be less direct by using the timeline retrospective. Have the team map out events and decisions on the wall using stickies and markers. Once they've built the timeline, use a different color sticky and have the team label the events with the name of the person who made the final decision. Once the team gathers the data, do some quick counts and discuss the implications of the results.

If it looks like the team isn't making decisions about their work, brainstorm ways the team can correct the imbalance in decision-making. The revealing of where the issue exists will likely surprise your team. Be sure to energize them into action and empower them to own how they do their work.

The Rotating Scrum Master

Scrum masters have hectic days. In the morning, you could work with the development team by facilitating a difficult decision, de-escalating a growing conflict between team members, or providing some guidance on technical excellence in an agile world. In the afternoon, you could help the product owner craft the vision for their product, understand how to write clear product backlog items, or grasp what value means in the product owner's context. Your day could wrap up in a meeting with HR as you discuss team-based incentives instead of individual performance reviews as a means to improve agility.

Clearly, the Scrum master is a busy person who needs a specialized skill set to succeed. The Scrum master is an observer. Your job is to watch the team: how they work and interact with one another. You also keep an eye on how the outside organization is interacting with the Scrum team.

When Scrum is new to an organization and a Scrum master hasn't been hired yet, many teams try to fill the role by rotating individuals into it each sprint. Filling a short-term need with a rotational Scrum master can work until the team hires someone full-time, but rotating the role isn't a long-term solution.

If you rotate the Scrum master role, you're assuming that anyone can fill that role. But there are specific skills that a Scrum master brings to a team, and these skills require time and focus to develop. If the Scrum master role is consistently rotated, you can't home in on many of the social cues, bits of information, and opportunities that can allow you to help and provide feedback.

> ### Joe asks:
> # Does a Scrum master need technical skills?
>
> According to The Scrum Guide, no, and in some cases, technical skills could be a distraction—especially if the Scrum master finds the technical work more interesting than coaching, facilitating, training, mentoring, removing impediments, and the organizational change that comes with the job.
>
> On the other hand, technical skills could be a benefit to a Scrum master. If the Scrum team is stuck on a technical decision, the Scrum master could pick up on the issue sooner if he or she has some development experience. But the development team owns the "how" of building the product, and they have all the skills needed within the team to deliver the work.
>
> Being a Scrum master requires so many different skills that technical proficiency belongs near the bottom of the list of things to look for when evaluating candidates.

A rotating Scrum master will make sure that the Scrum events are held but will they understand why? Is self-organization being preserved? What about impediments? With the Scrum master role switching hands regularly, what's the incentive to work through impediments that are beyond the team's capability to resolve?

Consider the Scrum values in the context of the Scrum master role:

- Commitment: A Scrum master is committed to servant leadership. You lead through influence, not titles. Your commitment is to the Scrum framework and to ensuring that the Scrum team enacts and understands the rules.

- Focus: The focus of a Scrum master is on the team's ability to self-organize around their work. When self-organization is present, teams are empowered to do their best possible work. You're focused on fostering a collaborative culture and helping facilitate the team through healthy conflict and difficult situations.

- Courage: Being a Scrum master is scary sometimes. There are things you'll do to protect your teams that won't always feel safe. You have to act courageously and say no to practices that harm the team. Sometimes it will take courage to speak truth to power. Lean on your courage to act transparently when serving the Scrum team and wider organization.

- Respect: As a Scrum master, you're working with people who might be scared of the change you're leading. Always be respectful to those people.

Respect their past work, their successes, and where they are today in their journey of learning and enacting Scrum.

• Openness. Scrum masters are open about the things they observe and their feelings about how things are going, but they're also open to feedback from the team.

Can you, when you rotate into the Scrum master role occasionally, live up to the Scrum values? Probably not. What happens when times are tough and deadlines are looming? Do you abandon your Scrum master duties and instead act as a member of the dev team by lending your coding skills where they're most needed? Or do you embrace the Scrum master role and try to help teams look holistically at their system of work, and inspect and adapt as needed?

Scrum does one of two things for your team and organization:

• Empowers your team to deliver valuable products by the end of each sprint.

• Shows you why you currently can't deliver valuable products each sprint.

When the latter happens and the Scrum team and the organization need help, a dedicated Scrum master can make all the difference. The role is designed for coaching, facilitating, teaching, mentoring, and training people and teams on how to deliver. You are the defender of transparency; you help create opportunities for the product owner to make new and interesting decisions when new information becomes available.

Considering the cost of not being able to deliver—or perhaps even worse, delivering the wrong thing at the wrong time, for the wrong customer—the cost of a full-time Scrum master suddenly seems like a bargain.

Not convinced? Let's see if we can more precisely quantify the value of a Scrum master. When an organization first hires a Scrum master, they do have an initial decrease in revenue (they have to pay the person, after all). This initial expense is one of the most common reasons organizations give for not hiring a full-time Scrum master. But this decision is short-sighted.

The Scrum master has three levels of service: to the product owner, development team, and the organization. Let's examine each of these in turn.

Your service to the product owner begins with helping the PO effectively manage the product backlog. This includes creating PBIs that are ordered by business value. The techniques and practices this vary, but the time you spend doing this helps the PO optimize business value. You're also responsible for teaching the product owner how to plan product releases and get a return on their investment. Done well, serving the product owner contributes directly to increased profits.

The development team needs your help, too. Scrum masters remove impediments, teach technical and team skills, preserve self-organization, break down silos, encourage collaboration, point out technical-debt issues, and facilitate the Scrum events. The result: a more effective development team.

Finally, you also serve the organization. By providing Agile coaching to the organization, you can look at the big picture of not only how your team does their work, but also at how the wider organization impacts your team. You spot the issues and impediments both inside and outside the Scrum team that make product delivery more difficult. By fixing these issues you are raising the effectiveness of your Scrum teams. As the number of effective teams in your organization increases, the value that these teams deliver is likely to grow as well.

If someone is only a part-time Scrum master, do you think it's really possible for them to perform these three levels of service in a way that makes a meaningful impact on the organization? Probably not. Organizations that use a part-time Scrum master likely won't realize the full value and potential of a high-performing Scrum team.

The simple solution is to hire a professional Scrum master to serve your teams. If you can't do that, find someone in your organization who's committed to the Scrum values and servant leadership. Get them the training they need and support them as they learn how to be a professional Scrum master. But please, don't set up your Scrum teams for failure by not appreciating the value of a full-time Scrum master.

So Many Impediments, So Little Time

Here's a scenario that illustrates another anti-pattern we often see: The Scrum master isn't effectively dealing with impediments that are beyond the team's capabilities, and these impediments are growing into blockers that prevent the team from delivering a product increment by the end of the sprint.

The development team has raised concerns multiple times about the following issues:

- A test server has been down for two weeks.

- The staging environment doesn't mirror the production environment, but the DevOps team is too busy to deal with it.

- The organization is requiring that code reviews be performed by people outside of the development team, and the team has lost time waiting for other teams to complete these reviews.

- The architecture team is spending so much time approving new coding patterns that it's hindering their ability to make progress.

Perhaps this situation is caused by organizational dysfunction. Scrum master inexperience could also be to blame. Regardless of the reason, one technique that can help is to create an impediment backlog.

Find a place that's visible to the Scrum team and stakeholders where you list all the impediments that are holding back the team. List them in order by priority or severity and provide a regular update on impacts and progress. Review the impediments with your stakeholders, product owner, and development team. Facilitate this exercise in a way that allows the team to resolve these impediments as quickly as possible.

Strong facilitation is essential for this exercise to work. Facilitation involves coming up with creative ways to gather the team's insights. Then you can take these insights and find ways to model and distill them into actionable improvements.

Facilitation also requires knowing how to co-create with the participants. Get everyone involved—get them on their feet. Use stickies and markers to build the impediment backlog, but don't touch anything yourself! Let the participants move ideas around and generate new ones. Using an impediment backlog can enhance the conversation and help the team discover new insights and solutions.

A few notes about impediments: Impediments come in all different shapes, contexts, and sizes. They can range from a lack of funding for a desperately needed tool to getting support from an external team that isn't responding to requests.

You'll be tempted to immediately solve an impediment for the team. Resist! Consider these steps before taking any actions:

1. Think about whether this is truly an impediment to progress or just a temporary blocker with a workaround.

2. If this is an impediment, decide whether the team can solve it on its own.

3. If you're sure the impediment is outside of the team's ability to fix, then it's time to take action and help remove the impediment.

Every situation is different. But your team needs you, dear Scrum master, to navigate difficult situations. An impediment backlog can help you get the impediments recognized and resolved.

The Dreaded Scrum Lord

The Scrum lord is a Scrum master who acts like a dreaded team boss. These Scrum masters bring the hammer down on slacking team members. They assign tasks, set deadlines, and manage to arbitrary metrics. Servant leadership is replaced by a command-and-control mentality.

Scrum teams are self-managing and self-organizing. Using force doesn't play well in Scrum.

Here are the kinds of results that happen when the Scrum master acts like a Scrum lord:

*   Decrease in quality: A team that has an imposed metric and unrealistic deadlines is forced to cut corners to meet the new demands. Quality is the first thing to go in these types of situations. It becomes very easy for a team to decide that, in order to meet an unrealistic deadline, they must stop writing unit tests. Or even worse, stop testing altogether.

*   Increased technical debt: A Scrum team that's under continual pressure isn't likely to make good decisions. Over time, a series of compromises in quality and architecture will lead to increased technical debt. Ironically, additional technical debt will reduce velocity as the system becomes too fragile and complex to change easily.

- Demoralized Team: At its core, Scrum empowers the development team. Self-organization removes the traditional command and control levers from software development. Adding those levers back in through forcing task assignments and technical direction takes away the Scrum development team's ability to own their work. This is an excellent way to kill morale and cause your employee retention metrics to plummet.

Scrum masters are in a position of servant leadership. You're tasked with managing the Scrum process, not the team members. Part of your role is to promote self-organization.

Scrum explicitly gives power back to the developers. Respect this! The development team members know what they need to accomplish the sprint goal. Trust them to get the right work to the right people. Enable them to determine how to do the work. Rules and mandates that come from outside of the team often end up as impediments during the daily scrum.

The next time you give direction as a Scrum master, pause and ask yourself, "Am I serving someone else's needs right now or my own agenda?". It takes a lot of self-awareness to answer that question. It's vital that you avoid Scrum lord behaviors and thoroughly embrace servant leadership.

As an exercise in self-introspection, write all the activities you perform in a sprint on separate sticky notes. Then, being open and honest with yourself, create two sections on a whiteboard: one for service to others and another for service to yourself. Place each activity in the section that's most applicable and ask yourself:

- What can I do to better serve others?
- What activities must I stop doing?
- How can I change my approach?
- Are there any activities I could be doing that would lead me to better serving others?

If you're feeling brave, invite others to join in this discussion.

Turning into a Scrum Secretary

The Scrum Master acting as a Scrum secretary can take many forms. Sometimes it's by taking notes: writing down statuses and team activities during every Scrum event. They write down the entire sprint plan, the daily scrum outcome, refinement discussions, and retrospective comments.

Other times, it can take the form of bringing the team coffee in the morning and sliding a pizza under the door at night. There's nothing wrong with getting coffee for your team members every once in a while; that's nice. But if your main purpose is to feed the team and keep them caffeinated, you're neglecting the responsibilities of a Scrum master.

Planning all the Scrum events and keeping calendars up to date is another way you can turn into a Scrum secretary. Honestly, these are things that the team can manage, and that they should be managing as a self-organizing team. If their capacity is going to change based on someone being out of the office, that's something they should consider at sprint planning. It's not the Scrum master's role.

Move these tasks back to the development team and get back to the difficult work of serving the Scrum team and the organization.

Acting as the Janitor

A Scrum master becomes a Scrum janitor when he or she cleans up all the messes that happen on a Scrum team. If the team needs a change in one of their digital tools, the Scrum janitor is the one they turn to. This person knows every workflow and every setting in the system. The Scrum janitor can cite the number of every story and every task. Need a new story? No problem, the Scrum janitor will add it for you.

Physical boards can't escape the Scrum janitor either. Keeping the team board updated, the burndown charts current, and stickies in the right box are all fair game for the Scrum janitor.

None of these activities belong to the Scrum master. The development team manages their work, whether it's in a digital tool or on a physical board.

The development team manages their progress and keeps the work visible, not the Scrum master. If you find yourself physically moving stickies or changing the status in a digital tool, then it's time for a conversation with the team. Teams should use these triggers—status changes and sticky note movements—as a way to maintain alignment and figure out what to do next.

Bottom line, don't touch the physical board or the tools!

Coach's Corner

Becoming a professional Scrum master is a lifelong journey. We've explored the many skills the Scrum master uses during their day-to-day work. You can spend years improving your coaching, mentoring, training, and facilitation skills. So where do you start?

> \|/   **Joe asks:**
> ⌣
> ## Isn't Administering the Tools Part of the Job?
>
> Ryan says: "When I start a new consulting gig with a new Scrum team, I'm often assigned a Jira account on day one. By the end of day one, I've made sure to talk with the DevOps team and have my account disabled. If I can't get that done, I'll make sure my access is reduced to read-only. Tools are for product owner and development team to manage, store, and archive work. A Scrum master can read the results, but does not add, edit, or delete content."

Start with The Scrum Guide. It's under 20 pages, but it contains everything you need to know in order to understand and start with Scrum. Read The Scrum Guide once a month and take a few minutes to write about an aspect of the guide that stood out to you. Set a calendar invite so you don't forget!

As you write, explore how the relationships between the various roles impact Scrum. How do the Scrum values apply to each role? What could happen if you as a person play the roles of both Scrum master and product owner? Does Scrum even allow one person to play two roles?

Consider the Scrum artifacts and how each Scrum event offers an opportunity to implement the three pillars of empiricism (inspection, adaptation, and transparency) to one of them. For example, say your team is working on a website for a company that sells furniture. During a sprint review, the increment you're inspecting includes new search features for users, and the product owner discusses a new shipping feature a competitor just launched. Full transparency is on display as the stakeholders and Scrum team discuss what to do next and the challenges they may face in doing it. The outcome is an adapted product backlog that contains a new product backlog item to implement the same feature the competitor has developed.

Switching gears from this hypothetical scenario back to your real-life situation, think about what's inhibiting the optimization of the three pillars of empiricism to the Scrum artifacts in your current situation. How can you change that?

Many of the topics and patterns we discuss in this book started as observations we made while performing this exercise. Over time, you'll notice the way you think about and describe Scrum becomes more concise.

During your monthly reflection on The Scrum Guide, you can also inspect your beliefs about Scrum and make corrections where they've gone off track. For example, some Scrum masters train teams to use a Definition of Ready for product backlog items. We'll explore this idea in the Product Backlog chapter, but the point here is that the definition of ready isn't part of the Scrum framework. That definition-of-ready practice could be helpful to your team, but The Scrum Guide handles "ready" in a different way.

In the next chapter we'll discuss management. While management isn't mentioned in The Scrum Guide, working with multiple levels of management is essential to adopting Scrum. We'll explore:

- Management's role with a Scrum team
- How to work with managers who are new to Scrum
- What managers typically need from the Scrum team
- What Scrum teams need from managers

Understanding management's role on a Scrum team and how managers can add to a Scrum team's success will help guide your coaching efforts and give your teams a better chance of success. See you there!

CHAPTER 8

Management

Manager: Ryan, glad you're back from Scrum training. I have a few minutes, so tell me about this Scrum stuff that I just spent a lot of money on.

Ryan: It's a framework for delivery. There are three roles: Scrum master, product owner, and development team. Five events: sprint, sprint planning, daily scrum, sprint review, and sprint retrospective. And three artifacts: product backlog, sprint backlog, and the increment.

Manager: You've got the jargon down, but what does it mean for our teams?

Ryan: It means that the development teams are now self-organizing and self-managing. We inspect and...

Manager: Wait. Self-managing? If teams manage themselves, what do I do?

Ryan: You support the teams. The point of Scrum is to get to "done," and the teams decide how to do that.

Manager: Let's stop here. I've got to head to a meeting, but I have some serious concerns about Scrum that we need to talk about later.

In our fast-paced world, middle managers are getting sideswiped by the increasing rate of change. It seems that every day there's a new blog post about how management is no longer needed on Scrum teams, or a new comic strip about a pointy-haired boss acting foolishly.

There are many good people in management who played by the rules, advanced to their current positions, and have now had the rug pulled out from under them by Scrum and the changing rules it ushers in.

What often goes unnoticed is how this shift in culture can trigger a feeling of loss in many managers. They've lost the confidence that they know exactly how things work in the organization. With loss can come grief, and here's the problem: The first stage of grief is denial.

Managers who are in denial about their company adopting Scrum may try to thwart Scrum at every turn. Managers control budgets, have hiring and firing authority, and can leverage political connections in the organization to dig in and resist Scrum-related changes.

You may think that in this chapter we're simply going to go down the well-trodden road of documenting everything that's wrong with managers. But instead, we're going to focus on you, the Scrum master, and your responsibility to coach and partner with management and the rest of the organization to ensure that Scrum is successfully adopted by all levels of your organization, from the Scrum team all the way up to C-level managers.

Remember, as a Scrum master, you provide many important services to your organization both during and after it adopts Scrum:

- You help management plan the company's Scrum adoption.
- You lead and coach people (including managers) during the adoption process.
- You help everyone (yep, including managers) understand how empiricism and Scrum work.
- You serve as a change agent, provoking changes in the organization (with management support) that improve the way your Scrum team works.

It's vital that you foster positive relationships with management and leadership so that you can perform your role well. But, as we all know, that's often easier said than done. Managers are human, after all, and dealing with humans is tricky. If you're currently struggling to work collaboratively with your company's management, this chapter will give you some strategies that can help improve those relationships. We'll describe some common management-related anti-patterns and suggest ways to better collaborate with management.

Unprepared for Conversations

Managers have many concerns, including delivery, predictability, profit, and budgets. They don't actually care about sprints, retrospectives, story points, or any of the day-to-day minutiae of Scrum. This can lead to a serious disconnect between managers and Scrum teams. The dialogue at the beginning of this chapter is typical of how many initial conversations about Scrum play out: The Scrum master is focused on Scrum and the manager is trying to figure out how they fit into this new set of rules.

As a servant leader working with managers who are new to Scrum, you must put aside all of the things you want to promote and discuss, and instead figure out what management needs from you. This will help you foster constructive relationships with the managers you serve. Here's a real-life example of what can happen when you don't take your manager's needs into account:

> **Boss:** *Alright, Ryan, how do you think our planning and budgeting meeting with the product owner and finance went?*
>
> **Ryan:** *Painfully. I thought the product owner and I had created a good plan heading into it, but it just got destroyed.*
>
> **Boss:** *The plan isn't the problem. The plan is fine. You came in here lite.*
>
> **Ryan:** *"Lite"?*
>
> **Boss:** *You couldn't answer basic questions about the things that are most important to me: schedule, cost, and scope.*
>
> **Ryan:** *But those things aren't critical to the Scrum team.*
>
> **Boss:** *You weren't meeting with the Scrum team. You need to think beyond your team.*

This conversation had a big impact on Ryan. His boss was right. Ryan had been completely unprepared. He hadn't considered what his boss and the folks in finance needed from him in order to feel comfortable with the project they were about to start. As a consequence, Ryan couldn't answer questions about project's schedule, scope, and budget, which led to many more questions from his boss. The moral of this story: Servant leaders serve, they don't push their own agendas.

So what do you do if you've noticed that you and your manager(s) seem to be focusing on different things and not connecting well when discussing projects? Look at your calendar and find your next meeting with your manager or with the leadership team related to the project your Scrum team is currently working on. Think about what those managers will want from you during the meeting. If you're unsure, ask. Seriously, go and talk with them and ask what they'll need from you.

Once you know what they expect, create a plan for yourself that includes answers to the following questions:

- What do the managers want to get from this meeting?

- How will I contribute to this outcome?

- Which Scrum practices can I leverage to achieve this outcome while still honoring management's needs?

- What data do I need to fulfill my role at the meeting?

- How will I know I was successful?

This kind of preparation goes a long way. By being a partner with management, you can increase trust between your Scrum team and the wider organization. Trust makes our lives easier. And empiricism (which is at the core of Scrum) can only thrive in environments where people trust each other.

Expecting Too Much From One Conversation

Ryan and Todd have both spent time in management and leadership roles. It amazed them whenever people they managed showed up with large, risky, and not well-understood requests, and then expected an immediate answer. When confronted with big decisions, many leaders will naturally reject the initial idea and seek a smaller, less risky option—and that's in situations where they have an existing relationship with the person presenting the proposal. When there's no history or relationship to fall back on, managers are even more skeptical.

As a Scrum master, you need to build relationships throughout your organization. If you're having your first interaction with a manager about a change you're proposing, take it slow. Don't be like Ryan (at the beginning of this chapter) and throw around a bunch of jargon. Instead, ask the manager what they need from you. They might surprise you and create an opportunity to have *another* conversation about a concern that's important to them. Your job is then to show up at that next meeting and deliver on *their* need.

Over time, you'll build a relationship and establish trust with that manager. Once you've earned their trust, you may have the opportunity to suggest a slight change to a current process or practice. For example, here's a fun suggestion you can make if your organization uses the common Red, Yellow, Green status-reporting practice often found in waterfall environments. (Projects that are in good shape are green, ones with a possible issue are yellow, and ones that are blocked or in danger of failure are red.) Suggest starting all projects on red (instead of green) until your team has released a done product increment and gotten feedback from a customer. By making this small change, you can show management the value of customer feedback, small(er) releases, and using data to plan and forecast future work. Incremental changes like this one can help managers gradually move toward more Scrum-like ways of thinking, without making them feel overwhelmed.

Just remember that going from introduction to suggesting a change in a company process—even a small change—is something that needs to happen over the course of many conversations, not just one.

Not Being Curious about Management's Needs

We've all been there: You're working with a manager who is against adopting Scrum. They put up roadblocks and try to maintain control and oversight over areas that Scrum teams should handle for themselves, such as architecture, design, and testing. They'll often mandate technical solutions to the Scrum team, regardless of whether the team members agree that it's the right approach.

It may seem like the manager is trying to make your life as a Scrum master more difficult. *They aren't.*

Unfortunately, Ryan and Todd have both heard countless stories from Scrum masters about impossible-to-please managers who "just don't get it." And we admit that we've voiced these complaints ourselves. Eventually, we decided to take responsibility for such situations, and you can too.

If a manager is putting up roadblocks and resisting change, stay curious. Consider what would have to be true for someone to display the "difficult behavior" you're seeing from this person. If you've followed our advice from the previous section and have fostered a relationship with this manager, ask them what they are trying to achieve.

When the person gives you an answer, truly listen to what they have to say, and then pause before responding. There have been many times in our careers where we wish we had taken a moment before responding. If the manager says something about Scrum or the way a team works that goes a little outside the tenets of Scrum, pause—instead of trying to immediately rebut what they just said. Think of a question you could ask to get to the core of what they're trying to achieve. The question could be as simple as, "That sounds interesting; what does your idea make possible?"

Staying curious (by asking questions instead of passing judgment) is how you fulfill your role as a servant leader. In situations like this one, you're providing coaching to those involved in the Scrum adoption—specifically, a manager. Asking questions helps you get insights from the manager about what they really need.

Here's an example of how this technique once worked for Ryan: He was working with a manager who insisted that every Scrum team in the organization set up their team boards the exact same way. It would have been easy to instantly reject this demand, and argue with the manager about how this policy wasn't in-line with Scrum. But instead, Ryan paused and asked, "What does a consistent team board format give you?" The manager explained that it helped him understand how the projects were going—which is a totally reasonable thing for a manager to want.

This exchange led Ryan to invite the manager to the next sprint review to hear from the Scrum team and stakeholders about the project's progress. The manager attended the meeting and, afterward, decided that he'd rather get updates directly from the Scrum team during sprint reviews, as that gave him all the information he needed. And he agreed to let Scrum teams arrange their team boards however they liked.

Staying curious and focusing on the needs of others can take some practice. Take some time to develop questions you can use when you need to pause and remain curious. Here are a few more to get you started:

- Which decisions would you change based on that information?
- What kind of new decisions can we make based on this change?
- What does success look like for this change?

Even when you have a mental stash of such questions, staying curious isn't always easy. During their careers, Todd and Ryan have encountered many scenarios where maintaining curiosity was particularly challenging. Let's explore a few of the most common of these scenarios and discuss ways to navigate them.

Focusing on Resource Utilization

Remember our discussion of Taylorism in Chapter 2, Why Scrum Goes Bad, on page 7? If managers in your organization frequently ask about resource utilization, that's a clear sign that they're still influenced by Taylorism. The concept behind 100% resource utilization is a throwback to the belief that, in order to maximize efficiency, an employee's workday must be completely filled with tasks they need to complete.

We'll suggest some ways to work with management on their "getting the most out of people" concern in a moment. But first, let's tackle a secondary myth that arises when management has resource utilization on the brain.

Many managers think that a good way to keep workers busy (a.k.a. 100% utilized) is to spread the workers' time across many projects. This strategy has what some managers consider an added benefit: It means that managers don't have to make ordering decisions about their project portfolios. They can simply start *every* project they have slated in the annual budget at the same time ,and spread workers out across the projects.

We've spoken quite a bit about *you* being curious, but it's equally important to raise the curiosity of others. Transparency goes a long way toward dispelling this 100% utilization myth, and so does making managers curious about other ways of thinking. If you believe that management is avoiding making ordering decisions about their project portfolio, try showing them connections between corporate goals and the various projects that are in flight. Here are some steps to get you started:

1. Invite managers and internal stakeholders into a conference room to discuss goals and projects. If gathering them all at once isn't possible, seek them out one by one to get the data you need for this exercise. In the event you can't wrangle everybody, be sure to share the results of this exercise with all of management.

2. Create a list of the corporate goals that that your organization is currently investing in.

3. Summarize these goals on large sticky notes on a wall.

4. Next, create a list of every project and initiative currently in-flight in your organization, and write each one on a large sticky note.

5. Place each project/initiative sticky note next to the corporate goal that it supports. If it supports more than one goal, place it under the one that it's intended to impact most.

6. If any project/initiative doesn't directly map to a corporate goal, place its sticky note on a different wall than the one with the project-goal pairs. These projects/initiatives are likely ones that were created just to keep workers busy, not to further a corporate goal.

7. Ask the participants to reflect on how the projects that don't support the corporate goals could delay the delivery of more valuable projects. This can help managers see how trying to keep people 100% utilized can actually *prevent* corporate goals from being realized, and make them more interested in creating policies that focus teams around corporate goals.

Ryan used this exercise at a company in the Midwest to help stop work on *over 100* in-progress projects that were created just to keep people busy. Not surprisingly, with more people available and both management and the people doing the work having a clearer focus, the higher-priority projects began to finish sooner than expect.

When management believes that people should be 100% busy at all times, we Scrum masters have a chance to pique managers' curiosity so they can find new ways of managing work. On an assembly line (the kind of work Taylorism was designed to optimize), it makes sense to limit downtime and to optimize how much work people can achieve. But professions such as software development require knowledge workers, not factory workers. In order to successfully perform knowledge work, people need time to think and space to focus.

As we've mentioned, 100% resource utilization often means assigning people to multiple projects. For example, someone might be told to spend 25% of their time on project A, 25% on project B, 25% on project C, and 25% on project D—as if people can split their brains into quarters. Being 100% busy removes the ability for teammates to work together. Alas, this practice is still common today. Fortunately, some transparency can help managers see that spreading workers over many projects actually takes a toll on productivity.

Ask the members of your Scrum team to track how often they task-switch, and then share the results during the next sprint review (you invited management to the event, right?). Managers are often unaware of how much time is lost as people try to multitask. Presenting this info can help encourage management to rethink their 100% utilization policies. Real data often piques curiosity.

Better, Faster, Cheaper—Who Cares?

> **Boss:** *Look, you can sell me on the Scrum theory all you want, but if Scrum isn't better, faster, and cheaper than what we're currently doing, we won't invest in it.*

When Ryan heard this comment, he got defensive. He channeled his frustration into creating a presentation called "The Business of Scrum: Better, Faster, Cheaper," which he then delivered at many conferences over the course of the following year. The goal of his talk was to prove his boss wrong. Ryan was resisting applying common business goals to Scrum. What he should have done instead was actually *listen* to his boss and consider why his boss thought about Scrum in those terms. In other words, Ryan should have stayed curious. Doing so would have saved him a lot of time and travel expense!

Ryan's boss was simply using a different lens to explore the benefits of Scrum. Truth be told, after a year of giving his conference talk, Ryan was forced to agree. A moment of self-reflection led Ryan to think about why Scrum actually is better, faster, and cheaper than traditional ways of working. Here are a few reasons that he came up with:

- Scrum creates opportunities to make new decisions based on frequent feedback. That's better than past practices that valued completing a set of requirements instead of collaborating with customers.

- Scrum is faster than other methods or frameworks. It's faster at delivering value to customers because the frequent feedback helps you know when problems occur, which lets stakeholders get a return on their investment faster. And learning where challenges and risks lie as the product is built is faster for the Scrum team, too.

- Scrum is cheaper. Scrum done well prevents you from delivering things that customers don't want and won't pay for—in other words, waste.

In all honesty, if Ryan had framed Scrum in the above terms, his boss would probably have become an ally instead of an unimpressed skeptic.

Consider the conversations you've had lately with leaders and managers in your organization. Were the discussions centered exclusively on the Scrum team's needs, or have you acknowledged management's needs, too? Put yourself in management's shoes and think about what they consider important (such as "better, faster, cheaper" in Ryan's scenario). How can Scrum create success for them and fulfill their needs? Stay curious and don't make assumptions.

Loving the Details of Delivery

By design, Scrum empowers Scrum team members to make decisions about their work. The product owner is fully empowered to make strategic and tactical decisions about the product. The Scrum master is responsible for upholding the Scrum framework; serving the development team, product owner, and organization; and removing any impediments that block the Scrum team. The development team decides how to best do their work and builds high-quality increments of potentially shippable product.

The problem is that this decentralized style of decision making can be difficult for managers to adjust to. Many managers enjoy making decisions about products and how work is done. Managers are often reluctant to lose this decision-making power, and they may feel nervous because the manager's role in Scrum is unclear. In fact, The Scrum Guide doesn't even mention managers.

So what *does* a manager do for a Scrum team? A lot, actually. Managers:

- Set high-level, organizational goals for the Scrum team. These goals clarify the purpose of the team's work. Having a clear sense of purpose motivates teams, which leads to high performance.

- Help ensure that everyone in the organization is working toward a common goal. An organization won't get the full benefits of Scrum if various groups aren't all aligned toward common goals and outcomes.

- Define the boundaries that Scrum teams work within. Management sets organizational standards, conventions, and polices that can help people focus and clearly understand how they should perform their work.

- Preserve self-organization. A manager should defend a team's ability to self-organize and decide how best to do their work. For example, a director in an organization where Todd was consulting tried to mandate that every development team create estimates the same way. A development manager fought for each development team's right to estimate the way they considered best. The manager eventually prevailed, preserving the development teams' ability to make decisions that enabled self-organization.

- Remove organizational impediments. In collaboration with the Scrum master, a manager should work to get organizational impediments removed as quickly as possible. For instance, what if your team only had one license for a tool that was critical for them to properly test an application? You could reach out to your manager for help expediting the procurement process for additional licenses.

- Handle HR responsibilities. These include policy compliance, benefits, career growth, training, and everything else related to serving the needs of their team members.

Managers are still very much needed in Scrum. Helping them understand how they can contribute to your Scrum team is an essential first step to getting them comfortable with adopting Scrum. Even after an organization has been using Scrum for a while, the Scrum master's work with management doesn't stop. You need to continually foster open lines of communication with management.

Pop the Scrum bubble that you work within. Step up and coach the outside organization on Scrum. Many of the managers you coach will have limiting beliefs that hold them back, such as "this is the way we've always done things." Such thinking can be so deeply ingrained that they may need your help to see that these beliefs are stopping them from moving away from Taylorism and into the digital age.

Powerful questions can help foster productive discussions with managers who aren't real keen on Scrum. Such questions bring clarity to difficult situations while also energizing people to take action. Typically, a powerful question is open-ended (meaning it can't be answered with a simple yes or no), direct, and focused. Most importantly, powerful questions are rooted in honest curiosity. Here are some examples of powerful questions that you can try when talking to managers who are skeptical of Scrum:

- How can we turn your concerns into an experiment?
- What do we risk by trying some experiments?
- What has worked in the past that we can build on?

Removing the limiting beliefs of managers (and others) and energizing them to action can help make your organization more supportive of Scrum.

Difficult situations involving management come up frequently. The techniques and practices that your Scrum team is applying—especially the transparency, inspection, and adaptation—can feel threatening to people who aren't used to working in a way that's open and transparent. But by staying curious and finding out what your managers need to feel more comfortable with Scrum, you can help them become more accepting of this exciting new way of working.

Coach's Corner

How long has it been since you've worked with the management team at your company? If it's been a while, perhaps it's time to host an activity that will not only generate some revealing discussions but can also help create a list of impediments for you and the management team to focus on. Here's what you can do:

1. Gather the management team into a large room that has plenty of space on the walls. Label one area of a wall "Why Scrum?"

2. Ask each participant to write their answer to the following question on a sticky note: "Why are we adopting Scrum?"

3. After everyone has written down their answer, have each person read their answer out loud (one at a time), and then post their answer in the "Why Scrum?" space.

4. Once every answer is posted, ask everyone to work together to group the answers into common themes. While every organization is different, there are some common patterns that will likely appear. For example, you'll probably see a grouping of sticky notes related to either predictability or delivery.

5. Review the groupings and select the sticky that best relates to delivery. For example, you might see a sticky note about code quality, improving development skills, understanding what your customers want, getting software to customers faster, or saving money.

6. Place this sticky note in a new area of the wall labeled "Delivery" and then ask, "Why is delivery hard?"

7. Give the participants a minute to write down as many ideas as possible on sticky notes, one answer per sticky.

8. Ask the participants to find a partner and, for two minutes, compare their lists and continue to expand upon them. You want them to come up with as many ideas as possible on separate stickies. They should also eliminate any duplicates.

9. Ask each pair of people to find another pair to work with, then have these groups of four spend four minutes comparing and adding to their lists of ideas. Have them write each new idea they come up with on a new sticky note. Again, have them eliminate any duplicates.

10. Have each group read their ideas out loud as they place them in the "Delivery" area that you created. If another group hears an idea they also wrote down, ask them to crumple up their note to eliminate duplicates.

11. Congratulate the group on creating a list of impediments to delivery.

At this point you have quite a few options. For example, you could have the group sort the sticky notes by internal teams or divisions. You could also invite the Scrum team(s) to review the list of impediments and add their own. In any case, this list should become the highest priority for the management team if they truly want to improve the Scrum teams' ability to deliver high-quality products. Help them order this list, and collaborate with them on solutions.

In the next chapter we'll discuss the sprint, which is the container event that holds all other Scrum events. It's a powerful constraint that helps Scrum teams deliver a product increment in a four weeks or less. We'll show you how to leverage sprints to best benefit your team.

CHAPTER 9

Thinking in Sprints

In 2016, Todd got a call from a product owner who was struggling. His Scrum team was using five-week sprints, with four weeks designated for work and the last week dedicated to retrospectives and planning. You might be thinking this way of doing sprints isn't actually Scrum, and you'd be right. Per The Scrum Guide, sprints are limited in duration to one calendar month or less, and committing a week to retrospectives and planning is highly unusual.

The product owner in this situation was having a really tough time. She had no transparency into the sprint backlog and couldn't forecast a release plan or make even basic assumptions about the progress being made on the work. The planning/retrospective week was especially painful for her: There were long meetings, lots of indecision and arguments, and she had little ability to forecast the next sprint. Most importantly to the PO, she had no idea of how to set stakeholder expectations.

As Todd dug in and started asking questions, he discovered that the product owner wasn't the only one in pain. Everybody on the Scrum team was miserable. Development team members felt lost and often didn't know what to work on next. Some had nothing to do the first two weeks of a sprint and then got slammed the last two weeks, putting in overtime to finish their work. The opposite was true for others on the dev team.

Daily scrums were status meetings, and often ran 45 minutes to an hour as the Scrum master showed up with a list of tasks to check on. The Scrum master didn't know Scrum; he was simply thrust into the position because he had a project management background, and the organization's management team had set the expectation that everything needed to be accomplished in an agile way.

The fix was simple and effective (although, due to the organization's culture, it was difficult to implement): They just needed to start *truly* using Scrum.

All the required Scrum events (sprint, sprint planning, daily scrum, sprint review, and sprint retrospective) are time-boxed. The duration of each event should be tailored to your environment. Here are The Scrum Guide's guidelines on how long each event should last:

- Sprint - one month or less

- Sprint Planning - a maximum of eight hours for a one-month sprint, usually shorter for shorter sprint lengths

- Daily Scrum - a maximum of 15 minutes regardless of sprint length

- Sprint Review - a maximum of four hours for a one-month sprint, usually less for shorter sprint lengths

- Sprint Retrospective - a maximum of three hours for a one-month sprint, usually less for shorter sprint lengths

The sprint length determines how often you receive feedback about your product increment, and the cadence and frequency of all the other Scrum events. The sprint is a powerful tool for a Scrum team that is often misunderstood and misused. Consider the following benefits of sprints:

- The sprint time box creates focus on doing only the things that are essential to completing the sprint goal, and getting features released to your customers. Any distractions that are not related to your sprint goal become an easy "no"—you don't have time to waste.

- Working and thinking in sprints will expose many problems with the way your Scrum team currently works. Every bottleneck, inefficient process, and ineffective practice will come to light as the team tries to get a feature completed, tested, integrated, and deployed by the end of the sprint. This provides excellent opportunities for your team to identify and resolve impediments that could have gone undetected or unresolved if you were using another framework or methodology.

- The sprint represents a commitment to Scrum. By working in sprints, the team has decided to provide multiple opportunities to inspect and adapt progress toward the sprint goal. This commitment allows the team to get feedback frequently and maintain alignment with the customers' needs.

- Working in sprints gives your business partners transparency into the team's progress, and empowers the stakeholders to manage cost and release schedules with real data, clear information, and product increments to inspect at the end of every sprint.

- Sprints give your team members opportunities to let go of limiting beliefs about what is possible and to try new approaches. While this may be uncomfortable at times, with the help of the Scrum master (you!), they can move through these situations and grow as developers and team members. The momentary discomfort is worth the long-term benefits.

The sprint is the container for all the other Scrum events. Understanding the purpose of the sprint, knowing common pitfalls to avoid, and understanding how to avoid them is pivotal to the success of your Scrum team.

We Need a Special Sprint

Some teams that are new to Scrum have trouble moving away from waterfall-style techniques such as phase gates and big upfront planning. Specialized sprints can be appealing to such teams because they model old, familiar processes and behaviors that have been in place for many years. But if any of the following specialized sprints sound familiar or even just tempting, your Scrum team or organization may have underlying issues that you need to work on.

- Sprint Zero - Also called architecture or planning sprints, the intent of this type of sprint is to create a robust plan, often in the form of a product backlog, that the team can use to get started.

- Design Sprints - The result of these sprints is a design output such as user experience or architecture. There's no business value delivered during these sprints, only a vision of what future business value *might* look like, such as user interface mockups or a database design.

- Development Sprints - Sprints where the only thing achieved is writing code. All other tasks, such as design, testing, and integration, are put on hold or handled by other teams.

- Test Sprints - Sprints where code written by another team is tested. Bugs and issues that are found are reported back to the team that created them.

- Integration Sprints - The output is code merges or attempts at completing integrations with other systems that the system is dependent upon.

- Hardening Sprints - These are for code clean up, bug fixes, integration, testing and anything left over, to make sure the system is ready for production.

- Release Sprints - Often used as the final phase, a release sprint is where software that has been designed, written, and tested meets the infrastructure team for deployment into production.

- Bug Sprints - After code is shipped into production and bugs start rolling in, these sprints are designed to patch and fix them, and then deploy those fixes back into production.

These specialized sprints all map back to waterfall-style techniques. In a waterfall world, you perform big up-front design (BUFD) work to define the product and requirements in a design phase. Then you move into an architecture and infrastructure phase, followed by a development phase. Hopefully, the testing, integration, and hardening phases come next. Then you finish up with a release phase and ship the product to production. During a post-production phase, you squash the bugs as they're reported.

Scrum is different. The sprint is a boundary. Within a sprint, the Scrum team performs sprint planning, the daily scrum, the development work, the sprint review, and the sprint retrospective. The outcome of a sprint is a production-ready increment of the product. These increments can be a major competitive advantage because, in four weeks or less, you have production-ready software. The next sprint begins right after the end of the previous sprint. *All* of the phases of each project occur within a sprint. If it helps, think of a sprint as a mini-project where the work is asynchronously executed by the development team. By the end, your team must yield a valuable and potentially releasable increment, no matter how small.

Sprint zero is one of the most popular specialized sprints. Teams often claim they need a sprint zero to take care of things that needs to be done before the first sprint of a project can begin. For example, a team might claim that they need a full product backlog before they begin the first sprint.

The problem with having a sprint zero is that the team establishes a precedent of allowing special types of sprints that don't deliver business value. If the development team's goal for a sprint is creating a product backlog, they're obviously not delivering a potentially releasable increment during that sprint. When business value isn't on the line, teams can be tempted to extend sprint zero a few days, weeks, or months. As a Scrum master, if you allow these behaviors, you're opening the door to the team using similar arguments in the future when delivery is on the line.

> ### Joe asks:
> ## What do I need to start a sprint?
>
> Scrum doesn't prescribe what you need to have in place to begin your first sprint. All you need to get started with sprint planning is a product owner, a development team, and a few high-level product backlog items. Is this ideal? No. But these roles and artifacts are enough to get started initially.
>
> Once you get started, you'll find out a lot of things that you had no way of knowing —valuable info that no amount of planning or studying could have unearthed. So don't fear getting started, fear *not* starting at all.

Figuring out why your team is asking for specialized sprints is the first step in removing these events from your Scrum practice. Here are some common underlying issues that can cause teams to request specific, specialized sprints:

- Sprint zero is a sign of a team that's looking to do too much analysis prior to getting started, and that is not open to learning during the first sprint. Teams also use sprint zeros to build a pause into the software development process to catch up on testing, technical debt, or to simply get an easier week to recharge and prepare for the next sprint.

- Design sprints hint at a team that's uncomfortable working with incomplete information. A hard truth in the software development world is that you can't perfectly plan complexity. You will experiment, learn, and adapt throughout each sprint.

- Test, integration, and hardening sprints are attempts to cram quality into the product toward the end of the development cycle. Quality must be a primary consideration on a Scrum team. The development team tests, integrates, and improves the product every day of the sprint—not just at the end. Scrum requires that, each sprint, the team outputs a potentially releasable increment, and that requires testing.

- Release sprints give the Scrum team time to move the latest product increment to production and verify that everything still works as expected. Often the team needs this phased approach due to manual deployment and regression testing practices. Any time the team spends manually deploying a product is time they're not spending building something of value that the business wants. To help your team move past these antiquated practices and improve efficiency, map out your release process as a team, and look for ways to automate repetitive and complicated tasks.

- Bug sprints are a sign of low quality. Slow down, take fewer product backlog items into your sprint, strengthen your definition of done, and stop creating bugs. Sometimes you have to go slow to eventually deliver sooner.

I Believed in Hardening Sprints

by: Todd Miller

Many years ago, as a Scrum master, I actually recommended the use of hardening sprints to a development team that was building a sales engineering tool. They were struggling to get testing completed during sprints. After every three sprints, we would do a hardening sprint prior to a release. I went as far as recommending a hardening backlog where the team would place items that they wanted to refactor and retest.

After several sprints, the team noticed a detrimental pattern emerging: Our hardening backlog was becoming larger and larger, and we could never complete it during the hardening sprints. We also noticed a sharp increase in the number of bugs being reported in production. During a retrospective, the team decided to ditch hardening sprints because they felt like it was causing a decrease in quality. Instead, they fine-tuned their definition of "done" so that unfinished work no longer accumulated. Harsh lesson learned!

Get to the root of the impediments that specialized sprints are covering up, and use the Scrum values to see your way to using sprints as they were intended: to time-box the end-to-end delivery of value to your customers.

Let's Change the Sprint Length

A sprint's duration is limited to one calendar month or less. Keeping the duration of a sprint consistent during a development effort establishes a cadence. A consistent time box also helps the team provide consistent forecasts to the product owner and stakeholders. And it offers the Scrum team a way to easily interpret a consistent set of data around how the team works and the complexities they're facing.

Once a sprint has started, its length can't change. We don't make them shorter because we completed all of our work done sooner, and we don't make them longer because we're not quite done. Once we decide a sprint length or set a cadence, it's a rhythm, it's a heartbeat, it's how we space out our feedback loops. Consistency is key.

The issue with extending a sprint is that continually extending it just one more day increases the risk of moving in the wrong direction, because you're not getting feedback as often as needed. You also avoid inspecting why the team struggled to deliver value at the end of the sprint. These impediments to delivery won't go away on their own and, if left unresolved, will compound in cost, delays, and risk.

> ### Joe asks:
> ## But we're so close! Can't we add a few days to the sprint to finish up one last product backlog item?
>
> Nope. Not even if you've hit the end of your two-week sprint and aren't quite done with the product increment. That's a difficult spot, but you have to go to the sprint review and discuss what happened during the sprint and why you don't have a done increment of product to inspect. We do not exceed the time box—no matter what.
>
> There's no such thing as a failed sprint, just an undesired outcome that we can learn from with stakeholders.

And what if the extra day you request isn't enough? How many times have you seen "just one more day" turn into "just one more month"?

The sprint is a creative constraint. Every issue within our organization that prevents, delays, or inhibits delivery will come forward quickly because of the sprint time box. The urgency to deliver, coupled with the necessity to improve, drives Scrum teams to become creative at solving problems.

Why does this matter? A sprint is a fixed period of time that you've decided to use to capitalize on an opportunity in the marketplace. You're delivering the right feature at the right time for the right customer. You're opening up the opportunity for the product owner to get validation for the assumptions they've made about value. The increments created each sprint are opportunities for the product owner (and the organization as a whole) to realize a return on their investment in the product.

You're going to find problems within your processes. Development practices will need refinement. Meanwhile, you're still on the hook to deliver features by the end of the sprint. This positive sense of urgency leads to improvements that allow you to meet the definition of done and deliver features by the end of the sprint.

If you extend a sprint, you rob the team of the opportunity to improve their process, practices, and collaboration. Stick to the time box and use it to drive continuous improvement and delivery.

Ask yourself and the team honestly, "Are we extending the sprint to meet an artificial goal or to meet a metric?" Address the underlying issues of why you're not accomplishing your sprint goals. Removing the impediments to delivery will pay off far better than extending a sprint to game a metric, or make it look like you delivered a done increment within the sprint.

> **Joe asks:**
> # What is the "right" sprint length?
>
> When the team is deciding on a sprint length, your first consideration should be how long it's safe for the product owner to go without feedback from their stakeholders and customers. In highly complex environments, an overly long feedback loop could be risky.
>
> Your team needs to discuss the product and technical implications of various sprint length options, and determine how long they're comfortable going without feedback, and how long the stakeholders are comfortable going without inspecting the latest product increment. Of course, the sprint duration also has to be technically feasible so that "done" work can be completed in its entirety.
>
> The number of weeks that your team decides on isn't nearly as important as the reasoning behind the choice and the collaborative discussions that led to that decision. Before your team decides on "just right", make sure you've balanced risk, delivering value frequently to your customers, and technical feasibility.

Scrum Has Too Many Meetings

The Scrum events fit nicely into a sprint. Sprint planning, the daily scrum, sprint review, and sprint retrospective are all time-boxed, meaning they have a maximum duration that the team can't exceed. Here's an example of what the events in a one-month sprint might look like; you can tailor the duration of these events to suit your situation:

M	Tu	W	Th	Fr
Sprint Planning	Daily Scrum	Daily Scrum	Daily Scrum	Daily Scrum
Daily Scrum	Daily Scrum	Daily Scrum	Daily Scrum	Daily Scrum
Daily Scrum	Daily Scrum	Daily Scrum	Daily Scrum	Daily Scrum
Daily Scrum	Daily Scrum	Daily Scrum	Daily Scrum	Sprint Review / Sprint Retrospective

When you map these events out over a sprint, it doesn't seem like Scrum is meeting-heavy, but after a few sprints the development team members might start to make comments about Scrum being meeting-centric:

"There are just too many meetings in Scrum. I never have time to get real work done!"

"These meetings take forever. Our daily scrum is 45 minutes at minimum, I can't remember the last retrospective that didn't run over into lunch, and sprint planning takes multiple days to complete."

"Scrum was supposed to put the focus on the team, but it feels like the focus is on my calendar."

Let's look at some reasons why this happens:

- Violating the time box: If your Scrum events are going past the allotted time, you need to take a hard look at why the team isn't able to accomplish the goal of the event in the scheduled time.

- People on multiple teams: Developers who are assigned to multiple teams have to attend Scrum events for each one. Consider single-team assignments.

- Bad facilitating: The events are within the time box but the team isn't making adaptations. For instance, if people aren't engaged in a sprint review or sprint retrospective, perhaps it's time to change the format.

- Old meetings still on the calendar: This is the most common issue. Every Scrum event was designed to replace traditional meetings. If your development team is still bogged down by their calendars, it's time to cut some meetings.

Every Scrum event is designed to remove the need for many of the meetings you had previously. The sprint length sets the cadence for how often we're going to meet with stakeholders, how often the team is going to meet with one another, how they're going to work together—it creates all the boundaries and containers for the work to happen within.

The sprint promotes collaboration. We can use sprints to help management learn how to interact with the Scrum team. It's incredibly powerful for management to have the ability to see finished work, just as it is for the stakeholders, and that can promote healthy and positive ways of interacting with the Scrum team. So what does that mean?

As opposed to having management swoop in every day looking for updates, you can work with the management team to say, "Every two weeks we have a sprint review that you're invited to where you can see finished work. Oh, and by the way, we have a team board and we have information ready that you're always welcome to view."

By working in a cadence, having the Scrum artifacts up to date, having a sprint review at a regular interval, and allowing management to participate and see the work, you're helping to teach people how to interact with the Scrum team by using the Scrum events as designed.

Bottom line: Help your team members clear their calendars and get to work.

Using Sprint Cancellations to Change Scope

The product owner can cancel a sprint before its time box has expired, but taking this drastic step is disruptive. If the sprint goal becomes obsolete it could make sense to terminate the Sprint. But a sprint is short enough that it very rarely makes sense to prematurely end a sprint.

Sometimes the product owner will cancel a sprint to impose their will on the Scrum team, or do so as a kind of negotiation tactic. Yes, the product owner does have the authority to cancel a sprint; however, that decision is usually made in consultation with the Scrum master and the development team, because it's such a dramatic and destructive occurrence. If the product owner uses it as a tactic to negotiate scope or schedule, there are likely greater dysfunctions on the team that the Scrum master can jump in and help with.

That said, *never* canceling may also be an anti-pattern. If you surveyed a lot of Scrum teams, you'd find that many have never canceled a sprint. That's interesting because, at some point, it's likely that it didn't make sense to continue developing something for their product (especially if changing circumstances made the sprint goal unachievable), so canceling would actually have been the best course of action.

Just like unnecessarily canceling a sprint, continuing a sprint that will never deliver value can also waste time. And so, when circumstances change, even if you've never canceled a sprint before, perhaps it's worth discussing.

That said, canceling a sprint should be an anomaly. Be very cautious about using this nuclear option. The major disruption that it causes is rarely worth it.

Follow the Requirements or Else

A sprint is a boundary that creates the freedom for effective self-organization, and self-organization brings collaboration and experimentation front and center. Each sprint, your team should ask the following questions:

- Are we building the right things?
- Are we building the thing right?
- What assumptions have we made about the product?
- What might change about our product?

All these questions will come up throughout the sprint, and teams will learn the answers to these questions by doing the work, inspecting what they've done, and adapting along the way. The business will do that right along with the team, too.

But we often see sprints misunderstood as time boxes that follow exhaustive, detailed requirements that were defined far in advance of the current sprint, and added to product backlog items by the product owner. The development team is expected to explicitly follow the detailed requirements without questioning the product owner. We've seen product backlog items that contain hundreds of lines of text and have detailed documents (including finite implementation strategies) attached that give exact outcomes. Under these circumstances, interfacing with the business or a customer is frowned upon. As a result, the wrong thing usually gets built—and it's built the wrong way.

We don't mean that you shouldn't gather good requirements and have an idea of what you're going to be building in advance of a sprint. But the more time that elapses between writing requirements and validating them against customer feedback, the higher risk of building the wrong thing. Instead of getting too far ahead with writing requirements, focus efforts on creating smaller sets of requirements and shortening the time it takes to get a deployment to production.

A sprint gives Scrum teams a time box with a maximum duration of one month, where we can try things without massive risk and without any permanent damage to our business or our ability to deliver. The business gets a lot of freedom to experiment as well. For example, the business may not know the best course of action among two or three competing ideas. So, they could ask for a sprint where we do investigatory product backlog items on each one, release something to the market at the end of that sprint, gather some feedback, and pick a direction for moving forward. So instead of picking an option blindly, they get the option of making a limited investment on one sprint and see which approach could potentially be the best, based on real market feedback and not guesses and assumptions. That's very powerful. The worst case scenario is that the team learned a little bit about the problem space, they thought up a new experiment for next sprint, and we used up a maximum of one month of work.

The sprint limits the impact of failure to the time box of the sprint and provides lots of benefits and opportunities. But if we're trying to follow old, detailed requirements, we lose the opportunities that the sprint could create.

Coach's Corner

During a sprint, have team members notice activities arising that *aren't* Scrum events, such as extra meetings, delays, interruptions, blockers, and impediments. As these activities occur, have the team write them on sticky notes and place them in a common area. The goal is to capture as many of these activities as possible.

At the end of the sprint, preferably in the sprint retrospective, have the team sort the resulting sticky notes using the MoSCoW (Must, Should, Could, Won't) method:

- *Must continue* - things that absolutely need to continue, or the success of the product will be threatened.

- *Should continue* - things that should continue and which might affect the product (negatively or positively).

- *Could continue* - things that we could keep doing, but that don't affect the product.

- *Won't continue* - things that are a waste and that we shouldn't continue.

Once the sticky notes are sorted, have the team step back and consider what stood out from the activity. Ask them these questions:

- Is there anything that should be moved? If so, why should it be moved?

- Were there any major disagreements? If so, what do we do about them?

- Can we optimize the "must continue" activities?

- For the "should" and "could" activities, should any of them move to "must" or "won't"?

- Are most of our activities in the "must" column? Are they *truly* things that we must continue or do we just feel like they are?

- How do we stop doing the "won't continue" activities?

- Were there any hard decisions?

- Based on this exercise, what are the one or two items that we are going to implement in the next sprint?

- When should we revisit this list?

In the next chapter we'll discuss sprint planning—the first Scrum event in a sprint. An effective sprint planning sets the tone for a sprint. As the Scrum master, it's important that you have an intimate understanding of the do's and don'ts of this event.

CHAPTER 10

Sprint Planning

Development Team Member: Does Scrum ever end? I feel like we're running on a hamster wheel heading nowhere.

Todd was working with a team at an insurance company when he witnessed the following scenario:

The Scrum team was an hour into the sprint planning event and there was a collective feeling that it had just begun. They spent this first hour exploring the meaning of a single product backlog item. They clarified the user-story format, added acceptance criteria, and drew a mockup of the user interface on a whiteboard. After the development team estimated the item, the product owner became unsure whether the value was worth the effort and started debating whether the item should be built at all. The team was stuck.

This pattern continued with the next product backlog item. The Scrum master became restless and called for a break as the meeting reached the two-hour mark. The development team had yet to bring a single item into the sprint. The Scrum master thought to himself, "How in the world are we ever going to build this complex portal if we can't even create a plan for a sprint?!"

When the event resumed, the product owner was gone–he had to run to a meeting with stakeholders. The parting advice he gave was to "fill the sprint backlog and I'll check to see if I like what it looks like this afternoon". So that's exactly what the development team did. They quickly created a bunch of slapdash PBIs so they could end the meeting and get to work.

As development work began, there was no cohesion within the Scrum team as to the expected outcome. Issues surrounding the scope of sprint backlog items became the focus of most daily scrums. Fifty percent of the sprint was spent trying to define the scope of the work for the sprint. The whole team was frustrated.

Did that scenario sound familiar? If so, you're not alone. We often run across situations like this: planning meetings that drag on forever, product owners who aren't always available when the development team needs them during this event, and PBIs that aren't detailed enough to get the work started. This leads to chaotic sprints, low-quality increments, and strained teams.

The sprint planning event is the first event in a sprint, and the entire Scrum team attends. The output is a sprint backlog (containing a forecast and a plan) and sprint goal that the team can self-organize around.

There are two sides to the discussions that occur in sprint planning:

1. What are we building - The product owner comes prepared with an ordered product backlog. A PBI should have enough detail that the development team can consider it as a candidate to bring into the sprint backlog. The level of detail depends on the context of your situation. In some circumstances, a vague idea may be good enough. Others will require that PBIs be refined heavily leading up to the sprint.

2. How are we going to build it - As the development forms the sprint backlog, they collaboratively discuss approaches to the problem at hand. More work will emerge during the sprint—i's important to be cognizant of that. We want the development team to feel confident in what they are setting out to accomplish, believing it's possible and taking ownership of it. The plan they develop should be enough to lift them off the ground as the sprint starts. A fully detailed implementation that implies certainty is not the goal. The sprint backlog, consisting of a plan and forecast, are owned entirely by the development team.

Both parts of the discussion, the what and the how, happen recursively as each PBI is inspected and the sprint backlog begins to form. This is not a typical planning meeting as it requires an immense amount of collaboration from the entire Scrum team. We, as Scrum masters, are there to facilitate and bring that collaboration to life.

In this chapter, we're going to explore the sprint planning event and see where it can go wrong by examining the scenario we just described. This story illustrates several anti-patterns that you should try to avoid and which can lead to extremely painful sprint planning events. If these anti-patterns are already present in your organization, we'll suggest strategies for fixing them.

Marathon Planning Events

The team in the example scenario suffered through painful sprint planning sessions. They tried to define requirements for very generic product backlog items that they hadn't seen before. The time it took to figure out *what* to build left them no time to consider *how* to build it.

The rush to figure out the requirements during sprint planning lead to many questions. During the sprint, development team members sought clarification about what they were supposed to implement: They scheduled meetings, sent emails, and dropped by stakeholders' and subject matter experts' desks to try to get answers. This led to a lot of frustration in the organization as people outside the team complained about the constant interruptions the team was causing. The team spent most of the sprint frozen as they tried to define exactly what they were supposed to be doing.

While managing the product backlog, the product owner would add product backlog items with little detail. At most, he would include a title and put a few details in the description, but nothing more. The development team paid little attention to what was in the product backlog until sprint planning which caused this painful cycle to continue.

A painful sprint planning event is a sign of an unrefined product backlog. The product owner is accountable for the state of the product backlog, but the development team has some responsibility in it, too. Having a healthy product backlog takes two components:

- A product owner who manages the product backlog appropriately given the context of the situation. This could mean they are actively involved in adding, updating, removing, and ordering product backlog items. Or it could mean they have delegated some of these responsibilities while still maintaining full accountability for the backlog.

- A development team usually spends no more than ten percent of their time during a sprint refining the product backlog. These activities include adding details, estimating, decomposing, discussing implementation plans, and performing any other product backlog activities that are necessary to prepare for *upcoming sprints*. We call product backlog items that have received this kind of TLC from the development team "ready" PBIs.

Joe asks:

How much detail should a product backlog item have?

In the product backlog, items at the bottom and in the lower portion are typically vague, big ideas that are meant to happen in the future. As you work your way toward the top, items become clearer and more implementation-ready. But how much detail should a product backlog item have to be considered "ready?"

A PBI should have just enough detail that the development team can start work on it with a high level of confidence that they can deliver it by the end of the sprint. Too much detail captured too far in advance could have you building the wrong thing. Too little detail and the team might not be able to effectively work on that item during a sprint. If the development team feels like they have enough info to collaborate on a PBI and it can be completed during a sprint, then it's "ready."

Painful sprint planning events are common. Often, the Scrum team asks to skip product backlog refinement so they can focus on delivering "real work." Let this happen. After many years of fighting this battle, we 've found that letting teams experience a bad sprint planning session leads to powerful teaching moments where you can make the value of refinement meetings crystal clear.

To learn more about facilitating effective product backlog refinement sessions, head over to Chapter 5, The Product Backlog, on page 39.

Leaving Sprint Planning without a Sprint Goal

In the story at the beginning of this chapter, during sprint planning, the team worked through the unrefined product backlog, trying to define scope. And then as they executed the work, they struggled to find answers about the scope while also building the product. There was no overarching objective for the current sprint. The product owner and development team frequently argued when a sprint produced an unsatisfactory outcome.

This is precisely what happens when a Scrum team doesn't create a sprint goal during sprint planning. The development team has no clear purpose, and the product owner doesn't have an expectation they can discuss with the development team and stakeholders. In the words of one frustrated developer, sprints become "hamster wheels."

> ∖// **Joe asks:**
> ⏚̈ **What's a sprint goal?**
>
> A sprint goal is a singular objective that describes the purpose of a sprint. It outlines a business need or feature for the product. It's the Scrum team's connection to the customer during a sprint. It creates transparency and is a scope-negotiation tool between the development team and product owner. As long as you have a sprint goal in place, then the product owner and development team have clear expectations of each other.

So what makes for a good or bad sprint goal? Consider the following sprint backlog for a team that's expanding an online pet supply store:

PBI #	Type	Title
118	Feature	Add Digital Payment - Apple Pay
119	Feature	Add Digital Payment - Google
120	Feature	Add Digital Payment - Facebook
121	Feature	Add Digital Payment - Amazon
124	Bug	Dog owner recommendations showing cat supplies.
126	Feature	Add Shipping Integration - FedEx

Table 5—Example Sprint Backlog

The various "Add Digital Payment" items used to be a single item, but during the sprint planning event, the development team split it into four separate PBIs because they agreed that they can implement each one independently. Along with these four items, the dev team forecasts that they can also complete a bug fix and add an additional feature that would expand on shipping system integrations.

The product owner has a hypothesis that the addition of digital payments is something that will be widely used by customers. The product owner thinks customers will be eager to use digital payments, so she put that item at the top of the product backlog prior to the sprint planning.

Here's one possible sprint goal for this sprint backlog:

> "Continue adding features and fixing bugs for the pet supply store."

Can a development team rally around delivering this goal? Does it describe an overarching purpose to do the sprint? Does it describe a path to the customer? Not really. It's rather generic and could be applied to every sprint for this team. It doesn't tell the story of a value proposition that the team is working to complete, nor does it provide an elevating objective for the sprint.

Here's another possible sprint goal for this backlog:

"Add digital forms of online payment."

This is a far superior sprint goal. It's vague enough that it doesn't limit scope changes yet explicit enough that it provides the development team with an elevating goal to self-organize around. There are additional product backlog items in the sprint, but none as important as implementing digital forms of online payment. This helps the development team understand how to organize and plan their work.

To further illustrate the power of a good sprint goal, let's say that halfway through the sprint, the development team realizes that integration with the digital payment systems is much more complex than they initially thought. The development team tells the product owner that they're confident they can complete one digital payment system, and asks which one to prioritize. The product owner says to focus on Apple Pay. The second example of a sprint goal is flexible enough to allow for these kinds of course corrections.

 Joe asks:
Who creates the sprint goal?

The sprint goal is an output of sprint planning. It's a collaborative effort between the product owner and the development team. As the Scrum master, you should help your team create a sprint goal.

The work that we do is complex and no matter how meticulously we plan a sprint, the plan will change. Implementations can be harder (or easier) than expected. We need to afford ourselves the opportunity to be agile, and sprint goals like the second example do just that.

Maxing Out the Team

Remember the Scrum secretary we described in Chapter 7, Embracing the Scrum Master Role, on page 75? That person is making another appearance here. Here's what we've seen this type of person do more than we care to admit:

The Scrum team gathered for the sprint planning event. As the development team watched, the Scrum master dragged PBIs from the product backlog into the sprint backlog using his favorite digital tool. He stacked as many product backlog items into the sprint backlog as capacity would allow, in order to maximize utilization and keep everyone on the dev team as busy as possible during the sprint. (The product owner and Scrum master often pushed the dev team to "take on more" and to complete more work than in past sprints.) The outcome of this event was the dev team committing to finish all the work in the sprint backlog. There was no sprint goal, only a giant pile of work for the development team to complete during the sprint.

We have seen this kind of behavior many times—development teams driven by the product owner and/or the Scrum master to take more work and commit to completing that work. This arises from a misinterpretation of Scrum: Many teams think that during sprint planning, a team must load the sprint backlog with as much work as possible and commit to completing that work. As a result, daily scrums center around how to stay busy. Each sprint comes with a deadline of work that has to be completed. It takes long hours and fortitude to complete all the work by the end of each sprint. The quality of the product is low, and the word "value" seldom enters into the team's vocabulary.

The purpose of sprint planning isn't to fill the development team's "plate" so that the plate can be "cleared" during the sprint. Rather, sprint planning is meant to create a starting plan for the sprint which includes a sprint backlog, forecast, and a sprint goal. The plan that is created in sprint planning will change. The sprint backlog emerges: When complex work is started, additional work is found. The point at which a team knows finitely how long it will take to complete a PBI is when the PBI has been completed.

Maximizing utilization of employees is an archaic way of thinking that has negative consequences on knowledge workers such as software developers. It's based on the belief that we know explicitly what needs to be done to finish a piece of work. Centering your sprint planning event around maximizing employee utilization will result in:

- Low product quality because the race to finish items becomes the most important success factor.

- Low morale as a result of sprints becoming mini "death marches" and employees being viewed as "resources" instead of, well, people.

- A lack of ownership of the intended value of the product because "clearing the plate" becomes the problem to solve—instead of pleasing the customer.

- No room for innovation because there is a list of things to do and that list fills—or is larger than—the time the development team has to accomplish it.

- Instead of conversations about being effective and delivering a great product, the team's conversations are about maximizing the efficiency of individuals.

Planning to capacity leaves no room for the unplanned work that always crops up when the development team faces a complex problem. The giant list of tasks that need completing becomes the team's focus instead of the value they're creating. This way of thinking is often coupled with extrinsic motivators like annual reviews or bonuses. This further drives development team members to stay busy so as not to meet negative consequences. Your product will reflect this mentality.

Joe asks:
Is sprint completion percentage a good metric?

Sprint completion percentage is a metric some organizations use to see if teams are finishing all their sprint backlog items during a sprint. It bears no value in determining the effectiveness of a Scrum team. A team could finish all their sprint backlog items but deliver low-quality work that adds no value to the product. Conversely, a team could regularly not complete their entire sprint backlog but deliver high-quality, valuable increments. Bottom line: Sprint completion percentages are useless and you shouldn't use them.

This situation might be a reflection of organizational policies that have been in place for many years and can take many years to unwind. You have to start somewhere, so here are a few ideas:

- Make sure the Scrum team leaves sprint planning with a sprint goal. Advertise the goal and celebrate success in achieving it.

- During sprint planning, ensure that the development team, *not the product owner or Scrum master*, is moving product backlog items into the sprint backlog. This is a subtle way to create ownership.

- Resist the temptation to assign items to individuals during sprint planning. Give the development team the opportunity to collectively own the sprint backlog.

Letting Debt Build Up

Here's something that Todd has witnessed many times as a developer on Scrum teams:

A Scrum team sits in sprint planning debating how they're going to implement a product backlog item. It isn't an easy conversation because this particular item touches a very fragile part of the application. The Scrum team has known this for some time, yet nothing has been done to change it.

The product owner really wants this item to be done because she'd been hearing a lot of demand for it from customers. The development team doesn't feel confident that they can accomplish this item without breaking something that's already in production. They forecast that refactoring the relevant part of the code base could take multiple sprints. This is a conversation that has happened many times between the product owner and the development team. In the past, the development team has always heroically built upon the fragile code, increasing its fragility but delivering the feature.

But this time is different. The last time they added functionality in this area, a bug brought the product to a screeching halt in production, causing a sprint cancellation to cope with and fix the issues. They managed to cobble things together but they lost the trust of their stakeholders—and the team was scarred from it. The Scrum team is now in a pickle because they don't want to repeat that same production-halting mistake.

What if this team could go back in time to a sprint planning session where this issue was first discussed? Imagine if, rather than bolting new features onto the fragile code base, they decided to take the few days they forecasted at that time to refactor while delivering the new functionality.

Fragile code bases plague the software development community. There's no way to quantify technical debt nor to imagine life without it during planning, unless it's allowed to be fixed by the development team.

Conversations during sprint planning should include the "how": How are we as a development team going to implement this product backlog item? If there are signs that things are getting tough in a particular aspect of a code base, ask these questions during sprint planning:

- Is there are way that we could make that area friendlier to code in?

- Are there any automated tests that would cover the existing functionality?

- Is it worth working together in pairs to find a way to make the code more robust?

- What can we do to make this code less fragile?

Rather than ending up with a product backlog that has a bunch of "refactor" items, take on technical debt immediately when it enters the conversation. If there is technical debt, incorporate resolving it into a product backlog item that delivers some sort of business value. Don't ignore it or you may end up drowning in debt.

Remember that the development team owns how to accomplish the work: They decide what needs to be done technically, the scope of the work, and what goes into the sprint backlog. If the dev team takes a stand against shortcuts and technical debt, nobody can force them to do bad work. If more teams took this approach, the world wouldn't have so many technical messes to contend with. Professional Scrum teams embrace technical excellence.

Coach's Corner

How can you make your sprint planning event more effective? A lot of Scrum masters make the mistake of spending the whole sprint planning meeting with their heads buried in a digital tool like Jira or VersionOne. You're just trying to help, right? Actually, you'd be much better off turning your computer *off* and turning your full focus to the meeting at hand. It's painful to sit in front of a TV or projector watching a team try to plan using a digital tool.

Here's a great way to facilitate your sprint planning sessions *without* using a digital tool:

- Always consider the inputs to a sprint planning event: the product backlog, velocity, capacity, retrospective commitments, the definition of "done", and the previous increment.

- Print or write the "ready" portion of your product backlog on a single color of wide sticky notes—one product backlog item per sticky note. This is the "what" for you to consider.

- Bring a blank piece of paper and write "Sprint Goal" on it.

- Bring smaller, different colored sticky notes intended for the "how." These are the activities that need to take place in order for the work to be accomplished.

- Encourage the team to break the PBI down into a list of activities they need to accomplish to complete it; if they have any additional questions about the "what," they can ask the product owner for clarification.

- Create an imaginary line (or use a ruler) that separates the sprint backlog from the product backlog. As the development team puts an item into the sprint backlog, move the line down.

- Whenever someone moves a new item into the sprint backlog, ask, "Has a sprint goal emerged?" and "How full do we feel?" Incorporate the answers to those questions into the Sprint Goal paper and by moving the needle on the fuel gauge to the appropriate spot, as shown here. If answers haven't yet emerged, continue this process.

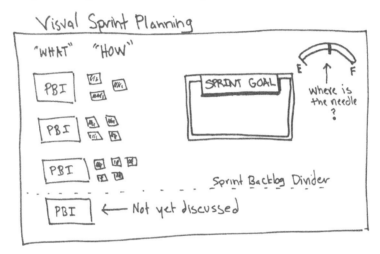

In this chapter, we looked at sprint planning and the pains that can come with it. Next we'll take a deep dive into an output of sprint planning: the sprint backlog. Hopefully, now that you're armed with better sprint planning techniques, your sprint backlog will reflect that. Keep reading to explore how you can continue the momentum of a good sprint planning event.

CHAPTER 11

The Sprint Backlog

As you may have noticed by this point in the book, we've been around, or part of, a lot of development teams. We were eager to write this chapter so we could take a deeper look at the day-to-day activities of development teams and point out ways to improve how such teams work.

The sprint backlog represents those day-to-day development team activities. Let's start our exploration of sprint backlogs by examining a situation Todd experienced while consulting as an Agile coach for an insurance company with a national presence.

The company had been transitioning from waterfall to Scrum for two years. (Yes, two full years of working to fully embrace Scrum. As you'll see, even after all that time, they still had a lot to learn.) In their software development department, by the conclusion of sprint planning, each person on a development team was required to have a minimum of 40 hours' worth of tasks, estimated per week in the sprint backlog. Tasks were to include development activities, time off, lunch breaks, and anything else that could happen during a work week.

Management had built dashboards that showed a summary of each developer's total estimated time for a sprint, as well as the actual time that person had spent performing each task. The timesheet system was tightly integrated with the sprint backlog management system—-Microsoft Azure DevOps was the tool in this instance—so every task and every hour needed to be accounted for so that the billing system was representative of the actual time being spent. Scrum masters constantly badgered developers to update their tasks in the system so that management wouldn't start asking questions.

Sprint productivity was a key concern of management and, in an effort to drive productivity, they created a metric called estimate vs. actuals. It measured the difference between the estimate a developer provided in sprint planning and the actual amount of time it took the developer to complete that activity. If a developer's tasks deviated too far past the estimate, Scrum masters were required to facilitate a conversation between the developer and the developer's manager about why the tasks were taking longer than the estimate. If tasks were completed *earlier* than expected, the Scrum master had to initiate a conversation with management so that the developer could be assigned more work.

Each development team as a whole was managed by a sprint burndown chart that showed a sum of all of their hourly task estimates and a trendline showing the remaining work. When the remaining work for the team was not trending in the right direction on the chart, the Scrum master was to bring it to management's attention so they could figure out what the development team was doing wrong. Adding new tasks or product backlog items to a sprint was particularly frowned upon because it meant a deviation from the plan created during sprint planning.

A vast majority of the time, developer and development team estimates appeared perfect on the dashboards, and their sprint burndown charts always looked like they were on track. But nothing was getting done on many projects: Software wasn't getting to production any faster than it had been before the organization started moving to Scrum from waterfall. Management brought Todd in to figure out why development teams weren't getting anything done and why they seemed so good at estimating, but bad at delivering.

Todd made a point to speak to folks across the organization, from managers to development team members. In these conversations, management's obsession with productivity became clear. Instead of owning the plan for a sprint and getting the work done together, developers concentrated on making charts look nice and getting tasks done by individuals. They spent a lot of time and effort making sure that their productivity metrics looked good—sometimes even fabricating numbers—so that management would leave them alone. Management didn't understand why developers weren't delivering anything and felt as if they were being lied to. The distrust between management and the development teams continued to grow.

Over several months, Todd worked with the Scrum masters and management to shift their focus from productivity to *outcomes*, which was no easy task. The key to making this shift was teaching the Scrum masters about alternative metrics they could use to quantify their progress for folks in management, about ways they could work with their Scrum teams and the organization to build mutual trust, and more about empiricism. In the end, the development teams gained full ownership over their sprint backlogs and started delivering. Management stopped requiring developers to estimate 40 hours of work every sprint and even abandoned their beloved burndown charts. These changes led to the beginnings of a culture that supported the developers in creating production-ready increments—instead of just trying to look busy.

The development team owns the sprint backlog, which contains the product backlog items that dev team members have selected for the current sprint. They add these items to it during sprint planning as they create an initial plan for the sprint. It contains a forecast of what the development team thinks the next increment will look like, outlines how the development team thinks they'll create the next increment, and provides an initial plan for accomplishing the sprint goal. (Remember, things can and likely will change as the development team learns more about the work). The sprint backlog should be transparent to everyone on the Scrum team. Exactly how to create this transparency is up to the development team.

(Don't confuse the *sprint* backlog with the *product* backlog. The product backlog is the product owner's responsibility and it contains all the details for the future of your product. The sprint backlog, on the other hand, is a much smaller list of PBIs that's owned by the dev team. It contains items that the developers intend to work on during the current sprint. The PBIs in the sprint backlog come from the product backlog, but the two lists are very different.)

The insurance company scenario illustrates one of the many sprint-backlog dysfunctions we've witnessed. Let's examine some other common anti-patterns that can arise.

Caution: Developers Burning Down

In our opening story, the development team didn't fully own the sprint backlog. Management dictated exactly how the dev team was supposed to create the sprint backlog and they put micromanaging mechanisms in place—constraints that created the illusion that everything was going as expected. The result was great looking charts but sloppy work and low morale.

You may find that management has a hard time coping with the changes that Scrum brings. They may search for ways to measure whether Scrum is succeeding. Executives often ask managers to find ways to prove that Scrum is working and worth the investment. They see the sprint backlog as the artifact that they can use to manage productivity and gain insights into how their employees are performing.

Not knowing any alternatives, managers often fall back on old ways of measuring performance that they've used for years (such as burndown charts and measuring estimates vs. actuals). Sprint burndown charts are a complementary Scrum practice that development teams can use as a way to inspect their sprint backlog. But we (your humble authors) have largely abandoned the practice because the bad behaviors we've seen associated with such charts far outweigh the benefits.

Our opening story described dev teams creating and updating sprint backlogs out of fear. In that situation, Todd overheard dev team members covering for each other and discussing ways to make the sprint burndown charts look the way management wanted them to. He often heard the Scrum masters helping out, clearly trying to keep management from intervening with the teams. The Scrum team spent a lot of time figuring out how to make their tasks and estimates create a good-looking chart. Teams went as far as cutting corners during development so that their actuals met their estimates. Sprints ended with a ton of unfinished work that was marked and displayed in sprint reviews as finished. Management had created an environment where the dev teams' priority was making the charts look good, instead of producing a done increment of potentially shippable product by the end of each sprint.

As we've said, the sprint backlog should be owned and managed by the development team. Whether it exists virtually or on a physical Scrum board, it's a shared workspace that the development team uses to continually and collectively plan and coordinate their work. It's where they create a plan that will help them, as a team, build a high-quality increment and achieve the sprint goal by the end of the sprint.

Our sprint burndown stinks

by: Todd Miller

I was a developer on a team that had been using Scrum for the better part of two years. During a retrospective, the Scrum team decided that, in order to better orchestrate our work, we would more closely inspect the sprint burndown chart during the next sprint. We had a monitor hanging in the dev team area that showed the current build status, so we added the sprint burndown chart to that screen so we could keep an eye on it throughout the sprint.

The developers became obsessed with having the sprint burndown chart trend in the right direction. Hour by hour, we did everything we could to keep it perfect. We rushed our work, didn't include emergent tasks in the sprint backlog, became competitive with each other, and worked independently rather than as a team as we tried to make the chart look perfect.

During a retrospective a sprint or two later, we discussed how focusing on the sprint burndown chart had caused us to act. We decided to remove it from the monitor and instead go back to using a physical Scrum board. The first sprint after its removal, we felt like we were back to normal: helping each other, working together, and not obsessing over a chart that didn't represent what we were trying to accomplish. We definitely learned that our obsession with the sprint burndown chart caused some negative behaviors.

If your organization's management team has become obsessed with the sprint burndown chart, shifting focus away from it is likely a sensitive topic, but one that you need to address. Often the best way to solve this problem is to offer them an alternative way to get the info they need to feel comfortable. (Ideally, a done product increment will become the primary measure of progress for your organization.)

Many of the teams we work with use digital tools that provide sprint backlog management capabilities. But we love physical Scrum boards and take every opportunity we can to teach development teams the benefits of using them. We discuss Scrum boards in Chapter 12, Reclaiming the Daily Scrum, on page 149, but we love the power of physical boards so much that we're going to promote them in this chapter, too.

In our experience, having a physical Scrum board is both wonderful for the development team *and* provides great insights to folks outside of the Scrum team, letting them see what's happening in the sprint backlog. We've seen this increased transparency cause management's obsession with burndown charts to fade.

Here's an example of a physical Scrum board that represents a sprint backlog:

When you suggest to the development team that using a physical Scrum board can be a great way to make the sprint backlog more transparent, you may get some pushback from people who feel that maintaining a physical board *and* a board in a digital tool is just duplicating effort. Don't force the dev team to create a physical board. After all, they own the sprint backlog and we, as Scrum masters, want them to take ownership of how they manage and visualize their work. Here are some benefits of a physical Scrum board that you can discuss with your teams:

- Imagine how much better the daily scrums could be if they're held while you're all standing in front of the board while actively changing and managing the sprint backlog as a team.

- A physical Scrum board really helps create transparency. If managers want to know what's happening, they can just come look at the board. (This applies to digital Scrum boards, too–they also increase transparency.)

- When you've been grappling with a tough task or product backlog item, it's really satisfying to physically move a sticky note from the Doing column to the Done column.

- As opposed to navigating a digital tool, glancing up at the board is an easier, faster way to double-check what development teammates are up to.

Ultimately, the development team decides how best to manage their work. If they decide to stick with a digital tool (a perfectly valid option), work with them to figure out how they can get the above benefits using their tool of choice.

Encouraging the development team to use a physical Scrum board is the first step in easing management's sprint burndown chart obsession. Once the dev team adopts a Scrum board, you'll need to continue to work with the folks in management to help them understand that the best way to cope with complexity is through empirical process control: transparency, inspection, and adaptation. (See Chapter 3, Breaking Bad Scrum with a Value-Driven Approach, on page 17 for a refresher on empiricism.)

The next time someone in management asks for a burndown chart, consider having the development team explain the physical Scrum board to them. This will give the manager new insights into how to get answers without disrupting the team. And hopefully, the board will include all the info needed to answer questions that your leadership team commonly asks. If it doesn't, that's a great opportunity to inspect and adapt the board to enhance transparency and build trust between the development team and the manager.

When dealing with complexity in day-to-day activities performed by the development team, organizations can leverage self-organizing development teams in order to solve tough problems. Obsessing over the sprint burndown chart is a form of micromanagement that inhibits development teams from truly self-organizing.

Changing the way your organization works is no easy task. You can help ease the pain of such changes by providing alternative ways to give people the info they need to feel comfortable.

Committing to the Sprint Backlog

As we discussed in Chapter 10, Sprint Planning, on page 119, the sprint planning event is where the whole Scrum team gathers to define the work for the next sprint by creating a sprint goal, a sprint backlog, and a forecast. At the end of this event, the development team should have a plan for the first few days of the sprint that details how they believe they can accomplish the sprint goal. That plan is in the sprint backlog (flip back to the intro of this chapter for details of what should be in this plan.) But many organizations insist on a more robust plan that leaves little or no room for change.

We frequently hear Scrum teams and organizations say that the sprint backlog is a commitment—that everything in the sprint backlog *must* be completed by the end of the sprint, and that sprint planning is the only opportunity the development team has to create a robust execution plan. This way of thinking about the sprint backlog shows that an organization is craving certainty, but certainty doesn't exist in complex projects.

In Scrum, the development team commits to achieving the sprint goal. But given the complexity of the work that dev teams face, it's impossible for them to commit to completing everything in the sprint backlog.

Have you ever looked at a problem and initially thought it would be simple to solve, but then started working on it and discovered that it was actually a monumental task? For example, imagine a bug that on the surface seems like it may only take a couple of hours to fix. But as you dive into the code, you find it to be something much more far-reaching than you expected. That "couple of hours" estimate balloons and turns into days or even weeks. That's the nature of complex work: It emerges, meaning that as you start the work, you find new work because it's impossible to predict all the intricacies of complex projects.

Let's think about why and how the sprint backlog emerges (changes) by examining what's in it:

- The What: A set of product backlog items that the development team has selected for the sprint, and an accompanying sprint goal. The PBIs contain requirements that describe what the increment may look like and what business value the development team intends to deliver to meet the needs expressed in the PBI. Bringing new PBIs into a sprint while it's already in progress can be disruptive, and should trigger a conversation between the product owner and development team.

- The How: The development team's plan for delivering the work. This may be in the form of tasks attached to PBIs that describe a technical implementation plan, or it could be the PBIs themselves. Remember, the development team doesn't *have* to create tasks—they're an optional Scrum practice that dev teams can use.

- A Forecast: An estimate of how much total work exists in this sprint and the amount of work remaining. Scrum is agnostic on how you estimate work. You can use PBI counts, task counts, Fibonacci numbers, zebra stripes, or whatever. We recommend *not* using hours because doing so implies certainty.

- Retrospective Improvement(s): At least one continuous improvement item that the Scrum team discussed during the sprint retrospective.

The development team needs to consider volatility when creating a plan based on the contents of the sprint backlog. Developers will come up with questions related to requirements and business functionality as they perform the work. The answers to those questions can change the dev team's implementation plan and forecast. And retrospective improvements change the way a Scrum team works and can impact how a dev team builds increments. So, as you can see, the sprint backlog is inherently changeable.

What's of utmost importance is that the sprint goal remains intact. You can have a new sprint goal every sprint, but once a sprint begins, the sprint goal must remain static for the duration of that sprint. If there is ever a circumstance where the volatility of the sprint backlog brings into question the development team's ability to accomplish the sprint goal, the dev team must immediately initiate a conversation with the product owner.

The sprint backlog emerges in the same way as the product backlog: It changes as the development team performs work. As Scrum masters, it's our job to promote the healthy emergence of the sprint backlog by helping the development team learn how to work under complex conditions. We must also work with the larger organization to make sure everyone understands that complexity is best dealt with through emergent plans. Although we need a plan, plans are never perfect and must be flexible.

So how do you go about changing this perception of the sprint backlog as a commitment? As a Scrum master, you should work to help the whole Scrum team *and* folks in the wider organization understand that the Scrum team is laboring in the complex domain of work. Way back in Chapter 1, A Brief Introduction to Scrum, on page 1, we briefly mentioned the *Cynefin Framework*[1] and the *Stacey Matrix*,[2] which describe various domains of work. We know this sounds pretty academic, but getting familiar with these frameworks can help you understand (and explain to others) why the dev team's work emerges. Here are four domains of work which are mentioned in both these frameworks:

- Simple: In this domain, explicit rules are defined upfront and, so long as those rules are followed, the outcome will be certain. Think about ordering a pizza for delivery: All the supplies come from the factory and, when an order is sent in from a customer, so long as the requests in it are followed, the outcome is certain—a happy customer.

- Complicated: In this domain, explicit rules are defined upfront, but they require experts to define them. Think about what it takes to build a house. During planning, experts need to plan the foundation, how framing will work on top of that foundation, electrical wiring, etc. If those experts' rules are followed, the house will be built correctly.

- Complex: In this domain, when we start, we don't know yet what we don't know. The best practice is one where the rules emerge and change as we go. Empirical process control, with inspection, adaptation, and transparency points, is required to change those rules. Software development falls under this domain.

- Chaos: When coping with the chaos domain, all one can do is act, sense, and respond. Emergency services such as paramedics, police officers, or emergency rooms fall under this domain.

As a Scrum master, you should be able to understand and describe these domains. That knowledge will help you give people throughout your organization a better understanding of complexity. It will help you have better conversations around the changes that happen in the sprint backlog, and how the plan created in sprint planning will change because of the complexity the development team faces.

---

1. https://en.wikipedia.org/wiki/Cynefin_framework
2. https://en.wikipedia.org/wiki/Ralph_D._Stacey

Update the Board!

Todd recently received this email from a former student:

> Hi,
>
> I'm new to being a Scrum master and I notice that our developers are typically not updating their sprint tasks. Oftentimes, I badger them to update their tickets, but they won't. So when we get to the sprint review, at first glance, it looks like they haven't completed any work, even if that isn't true. Do you have any advice on how to motivate people to update their tickets?

Can you relate to this Scrum master? Have you ever felt like you were the Scrum police, chasing after developers, begging them to update Jira? We certainly have. But is the development team the problem in this scenario, or are we?

Remember that the development team owns the sprint backlog. As we discussed in the last section, there can be a lot of volatility in the sprint backlog as the Scrum team learns about the product, and because the developers may find unexpected work as the project is underway. It's up to the development team to find ways to make that volatility transparent.

 Joe asks:
Who updates the sprint backlog?

Anyone on the development team can update the sprint backlog. No one outside of the dev team should update the sprint backlog—not even you, the Scrum master.

You can help the development team by emphasizing the importance of creating transparency in the sprint backlog. Here are some reasons why it's important that the dev team make the sprint backlog transparent to the entire Scrum team:

- During the daily scrum, a transparent sprint backlog helps the development team see how much progress they've made toward achieving the sprint goal.

- It lets everyone on the Scrum team knows where things stand.

- It provides a way to identify potential impediments to completing the sprint goal.

- It's a useful way for dev team members with different skill sets to coordinate work.

- It helps keep dev team members from getting interrupted by status questions from other developers and folks outside the Scrum team.

- It builds trust between the Scrum team and the rest of the organization.

As Scrum masters, we've made the mistake of harassing dev team members to update the sprint backlog more than we care to admit. We've even taken it upon ourselves to do the updating. But doing that actually makes the sprint backlog *less* transparent: It becomes a status board that's owned by the Scrum master rather than the development team. This negatively impacts the dev team's ability to self-organize because they have less ownership of their work.

Ryan used to update the sprint backlog for one of his teams but, after seeing some of the negative impacts we just described, he quit cold turkey. At first, the development team didn't seem to care, but they gradually started having problems with forecasting and answering basic questions that were coming up during Scrum events (specifically, the daily scrum and sprint review). With time and practice, the development team learned how to own and manage the work in *their* sprint backlog and started to communicate better with the product owner and stakeholders.

Here's the big takeaway from this scenario: We make an implicit deal in Scrum. The product owner agrees that the development team can focus during a sprint and not get pulled into countless status meetings—as long as the development team keeps their work and progress transparent. Ultimately, it's a win-win for everyone.

When you're faced with a development team that isn't updating their sprint backlog, ask yourself these questions:

- Are you asking the dev team to update the sprint backlog just for the sake of updating it?

- Is the development team gelling and working well as a team?

- Are you asking them to update the sprint backlog because stakeholders are demanding info from you about the dev team's work?

- Does the dev team understand the importance of creating transparency in the sprint backlog?

- Is the development team afraid of what could happen if their work is made transparent for everyone to see?

Why this self-reflection? When we've gotten irritated about our team not updating the product backlog, we've often found that it's driven by us wanting to feel as though we're appropriately serving the dev team. Although we had good intentions, by acting as the Scrum police, we ended up inhibiting the dev team's progress. In some instances, stakeholders were pestering us to provide status reports because they were still used to the old, pre-Scrum way of doing things. We realized that we were harassing the dev team for updates because we were worried about our own jobs, not about the well-being of the dev team.

Figure out what's driving your behavior and bring it up in the next retrospective. Be open (a Scrum value!) and explain to the Scrum team what's causing you to feel this way. Facilitate a broader discussion about the importance of creating transparency in the sprint backlog, and talk about the importance of the dev team owning the sprint backlog. Solicit feedback from the Scrum team and find a new approach that you can try during the next sprint. Although this conversation may not be easy, you'll likely be pleasantly surprised at the positive impact it has.

If you're a Scrum master who's currently struggling to get your development team to keep their sprint backlog up to date, ask the team two key questions, either at the end of or immediately following the daily scrum:

- What did we learn over the last 24 hours that could change our current plan?

- How can we update the plan with that new knowledge while keeping the sprint goal intact?

By reframing the task of "keeping the board updated" as an opportunity to reflect on what we've learned and how it impacts the Scrum team's progress toward the sprint goal, you can help shift the dev team's behavior toward more transparency.

The Daily Projector Update

All too often, this is how we see teams update their sprint backlog: Every morning during the daily scrum, the development team and Scrum master meet in front of a projector. The Scrum master pulls up the digital sprint backlog management tool and asks each developer for their status so she can update the sprint backlog accordingly. Dev team members stare lifelessly at the projector, waiting for their turn to speak. Very rarely does anyone update the sprint backlog at any other time.

Aside from the developers' obvious lack of enthusiasm, what's wrong with this scenario? First and foremost, the Scrum master shouldn't be the one updating the sprint backlog. The *development team* should update it as often as they see fit. At minimum, they should update it once a day during the daily scrum. And if they need to update it more often than once a day, they're free to do so.

All too often, we see sprint backlogs stay static after sprint planning—they become lifeless artifacts. Some dev teams *think* there's no reason to constantly inspect or adapt the sprint backlog, but they really should. Inspecting and adapting it should be the main focus of the daily scrum. As we've discussed, the plan the dev team devised during sprint planning will likely substantially change as they execute the work. Continually updating the sprint backlog to reflect these changes creates important transparency around the complexity of the work both for the entire Scrum team and the wider organization. Dev team members need to be the ones who do the updating because nobody knows the nature of the work as well as they do—after all, they're the ones performing it.

Obviously, development team members talk to each other outside of the Scrum events. They discuss requirements, technology, quality, testing, security, and all the other development activities. These conversations lead to trying new tactics to accomplish the sprint goal. These tactical changes should be reflected in updates to the sprint backlog.

Over the years, we've noticed that if we don't hear laughter in a development team's area every now and again, that's a sign that the dev team is operating more like a golf team than a basketball team. Golf teams are made up of individual players who sync up at the end of a tournament, hoping that they have the best collective score. Basketball teams, on the other hand, progress down the court passing the ball to the open teammate, working together as a unit to score points. Golf teams don't need updated sprint backlogs, but basketball teams do. Your dev team members should strive to work together like a basketball team—even if they're not into sports.

If you find yourself doing the daily projector update during the daily scrum, there's a simple solution: stop doing it. Go to work tomorrow and resist the temptation to touch the sprint backlog at all. Don't even offer to pull it up on the projector. Heck, skip the daily scrum altogether tomorrow and see what happens. Continue not touching the sprint backlog, and notice whether it changes.

Most likely, the dev team will start updating the sprint backlog during the daily scrum, and maybe at other times throughout the day. If you don't see them making any updates after a couple of days, pop into the next daily scrum and gently suggest they inspect the sprint backlog to check whether it needs any adaptations. But whatever you do, don't make these edits yourself! Leave it to the dev team members.

Waiting on a Miracle

A Scrum master recently asked Todd the following question:

> I've noticed that my development team members are taking forever to get a code review from the architecture team. It's wreaking havoc on our sprints because we can't consider anything done without having that code review. Any advice on what I can do?

This scenario is an example of how outside dependencies can block a development team. Clearly, the architecture team's code review was an impediment that needed to be addressed. To create transparency around the bottleneck that these code reviews were creating, Todd suggested the Scrum master work with the dev team to map out their workflow. She took his advice and, a week later, the dev team had identified each stage that a PBI had to go through during a sprint to get it to a "done" state. The development team then visually represented their workflow on their Scrum board and did a great job keeping it up to date.

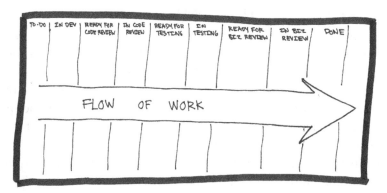

As the weeks passed, this visualization gave the Scrum team members insights into the development team's work that they'd never had before. It allowed the Scrum master to see a pattern of PBIs getting stuck in the "Ready for code review" and "In code review" columns. The Scrum master suggested to the dev team that they start writing the date that a PBI arrived in the "Ready for code review", "In code review", and "Ready for testing" columns so they could quantify just how long it was taking for the architecture team to complete code reviews.

By collecting this data, the team discovered that it was taking and average of five days for a PBI to move from "Ready for code review" to "Ready for testing." Five days seemed like an eternity considering they were using two-week sprints. The development team hadn't considered changing their code-review process or even treating it as an impediment because it had been in place before the organization adopted Scrum—it's what they'd always done. But bringing transparency to the 5-day bottleneck made it clear that the code-review process needed to change.

The Scrum master now had the info that she needed to discuss the code-review process with the rest of the organization. Speaking candidly with the architecture team, she shared the five-day average time that their code reviews took. They acknowledged that this was a problem but didn't know how to solve it, so the Scrum master and the head of the architecture team escalated the issue to folks in upper management. Faced with the data about the duration of the delays, and wanting to speed up the development team's progress, the managers agreed to a big change: They allowed the development team to start doing their *own* code reviews. After an initial adjustment period, the dev team can now perform the complete workflow for their PBIs—including code review—in far less time than it took when they relied on the architecture team. Everyone in the organization is pleased by the team's increased productivity, and the architecture team is happy to have one less task on their plate.

What we really like about this solution is that it also re-enforced the need for truly cross-functional teams. As we discussed in Chapter 6, The Development Team, on page 57, the development team should have *all* the capabilities they need to complete their work. In this scenario, that meant the developers needed to level up their ability to review and improve code.

Identifying their workflow could be just what your development team needs to take their sprint backlog to the next level. There are typically a lot of stages that a PBI has to go through before it can be considered "done," and identifying these stages can help unearth dependencies, bottlenecks, and impediments—including ones the team hadn't noticed before.

To understand your team's workflow, have the development team members work together to define all the stages that a PBI in the sprint backlog must go through to get to done. You can use the example chart we included in this section as a starting point, but remember that every dev team has a different workflow because of the specific product they're building, organization they're in, and their own definition of "done."

Once the development team has outlined their workflow, they can measure the *cycle time* it takes to complete a PBI in the sprint backlog: the amount of time a PBI takes from start to finish. When measuring cycle time, it's important to know when a PBI is active and when it is finished. At the conclusion of sprint planning, when the sprint backlog has been created, none of the PBIs are active yet. PBIs becomes active when the development team begins work on them. In our example workflow chart, a PBI becomes active when it moves from the "To-do" column to the "In dev" column, and it finishes when it moves to the "Done" column. If it's helpful, you can also measure the cycle time between each stage of the workflow.

Using cycle time as a metric can give the development team additional transparency into the sprint backlog. A team can then work to reduce their cycle time and look for stages in their workflow that are bottlenecks, such as the architecture code reviews we discussed earlier.

Once you've gathered some cycle-time data, you can talk to the dev team about the cycle time of their workflow as a whole and/or between each phase of the workflow. Inspect phases that have longer cycle times than others and try to figure out why. You might discover that the dev team lacks certain tools they need, has organizational constraints or outside dependencies, or even lacks a necessary skill set. Once you identify impediments, work with the dev team and the wider organization to remove them.

Understanding and measuring cycle times is the tip of the iceberg when it comes to new ways the development team can manage the sprint backlog and make it more transparent. Another technique we've come to love is implementing the Kanban method. Keep reading to learn how you can start using Scrum and Kanban together.

Coach's Corner

We've said this before and we'll say it again: The development team owns the sprint backlog. The sprint backlog needs to be transparent so the dev team can properly inspect it and, if necessary, adapt their plan for achieving the sprint goal. Such transparency might feel scary to some development teams as they may still be used to the pre-Scrum ways of doing things—which probably didn't involve as much transparency as Scrum requires. As Scrum masters, we can ease those fears by using transparency to promote changes that will improve the development team's workflow, and by promising that we'll work with management to tackle any impediments that are uncovered by the increased transparency. As we just mentioned, an approach that we love is having the dev team use Kanban to manage their sprint backlog.

Kanban is an agile method that provides a way of streamlining how value is delivered in complex projects. The folks at Scrum.org have created a course titled "Professional Scrum with Kanban" and the Kanban Guide for Scrum Teams.[3] Both provide great information for implementing Kanban principles, practices, and metrics with Scrum teams. We suggest you give the guide a read and see if it turns you onto any new ideas.

Now that we've examined the sprint backlog, it's time to move on to the event that happens every day and gives the dev team the opportunity to inspect and adapt the sprint backlog: the daily scrum.

---

3.   https://www.scrum.org/resources/kanban-guide-scrum-teams

Reclaiming the Daily Scrum

Every Scrum team has struggled with the daily scrum—it's the subject of endless misunderstanding. The daily scrum is a chance for the development team to plan how they are going to work together to make progress toward their sprint goal over the next 24 hours. In short, it's a collaborative planning session with a 15-minute time box. But in reality, it's often treated as a status meeting and/or an opportunity to solve problems. For example, have you ever witnessed a daily scrum like this?

Scrum Master: Alright, Ben, you go first. Anything to report?

Ben: Nope! Still working on ticket number 2831. Made some progress, and should know more tomorrow.

Scrum Master: Ben, that's three days in a row. Hopefully today is a good day. Okay, John, you're up. How's your task going?

John: Finished it late last night. Ready to take another task.

Emma: Hey John, that check-in broke the build and I haven't been able to deploy all morning.

Manager: That's the fourth time this month, John. Let's talk about this during our next one-on-one.

Scrum Master: Alright, let's table this issue for now. We have nine more people to hear from.

By that point, most of the other team members have checked out, and who could blame them? This disaster of a meeting could go on for another 30 minutes. How likely is it that John will share anything important during this or any future daily scrum? Could Emma have offered help instead of just voicing criticism? Why is the manager participating? Why are the developers giving status reports to the Scrum master? We will explore these anti-patterns throughout the chapter, but first, why is the daily scrum a valuable event?

The daily scrum is one of the most reliable indicators of the health of the Scrum team. If you know what to look for, you'll see that a development team reveals quite a bit about itself during the daily scrum. Watching a daily scrum closely could tell you enough to answer these questions:

- Is this a self-organizing team?

- Does the team collaborate on work?

- Does the team have a sense of shared accountability and ownership of their work?

- Is the development team focused on outcomes (the sprint goal) or on individual tasks?

- Is this an empowered team that owns its sprint backlog?

When executed well, the daily scrum is a great way to get the members of your Scrum team aligned with each other, inspect progress toward your sprint goal, and create a collaborative plan for the next 24 hours. It gives the development team an opportunity to make small decisions quickly. While inspecting their progress, team members can raise concerns, ask for help, and share what they've learned about the work over the past 24 hours. By embracing this level of transparency, the development team enhances its communication and collaboration.

But it's amazing how many different ways this 15-minute event can go wrong. If your daily scrum is a wreck, you're at risk. Your team's work isn't transparent, the team doesn't have a daily plan for achieving the sprint goal, and it's easy for the team to end up off course.

In this chapter we'll examine daily scrum anti-patterns that rob your team members of their ability to truly self-organize and plan their days. We'll suggest ways to reclaim the daily scrum and improve the overall health of your Scrum team.

The Daily Scrum as Status Meeting

Take a moment and consider how your most recent daily scrum went. Was it similar to the dialog at the beginning of this chapter? Be honest. We frequently see Scrum masters facilitate daily scrums by having each team member answer these three questions from The Scrum Guide, which on the surface seem helpful:

- What did I do yesterday that helped the development team meet the sprint goal?

- What will I do today to help the development team meet the sprint goal?

- Do I see any impediments that prevent me or the development team from meeting the sprint goal?

Unfortunately, these questions can turn the daily scrum—an alignment and planning event—into a status meeting. Why? Because the daily scrum should be team-centric. It's an opportunity for the team to collaborate on a plan around the daily work that will lead to them achieving the sprint goal. But these questions make team members focus on themselves as individuals, not as part of the team. When the focus is on individual status updates, you've lost most of the value of the daily scrum.

During this type of daily scrum, collaboration is typically low. Issues stay hidden, impediments go unresolved, and the team members are never sure how they're progressing. You lose transparency and put the sprint goal at risk because the focus is on individual statuses rather than on the development team's progress on sprint backlog items, or toward achieving the sprint goal.

 Joe asks:
What's an Impediment?

An impediment is anything that could prevent the development team from achieving its sprint goal. These are typically problems that go beyond a Scrum team's ability to self-organize around and solve. Some examples include:

- Lack of a vital skill set or key information
- Excessive pressure from management
- An absent product owner

People often apply the term "impediment" too broadly, using it to describe even the simplest speed bumps the team encounters, such as needing a meeting scheduled. These aren't true impediments, as they can easily be solved with a little brainstorming and collaboration.

To break this anti-pattern, you need to shift the focus to the work itself, rather than the individual team members performing the work.

No one person owns the daily scrum. It's an opportunity for the development team members to work together to develop a plan for the day based on their current progress, and on figuring out a path that leads to the best opportunity of achieving the sprint goal. By the end of the daily scrum, the whole team must agree on the plan and commit to working on it.

If the team discovers an impediment to achieving the sprint goal, they don't point fingers. The team members swarm the issue(s) and respectfully help those who need it.

Every person is responsible for achieving the sprint goal—you don't get partial credit for getting your individual work item done on time. The team succeeds and fails together. The daily scrum gives everyone a daily opportunity to align on what needs to be done to make success more likely.

So if your daily scrums are currently nothing more than status meetings, how do you guide your team toward more valuable, team-oriented daily scrums? Stop using the three questions we listed at the beginning of this section.

Wait...did you not know that the three questions are optional? It's true: *You don't have to use the three questions.* In fact, if your team is struggling to collaborate using the questions in The Scrum Guide, consider developing new questions that allow the team to explore the work collaboratively and form a plan for the next 24 hours. Here are a few examples of questions that we've used:

- Is anything stuck?
- If something is stuck, how can we all work together to get this work unstuck?
- Who needs help?
- What's the most important thing we need to accomplish today?
- How do we increase the odds that the most important things get to done?

Another thing you can try is using a physical team board and asking the team to walk through each piece of work in the sprint backlog. Facilitate the conversation to include everyone to get different perspectives about the progress the team is making on each product backlog item, and input on what the team could do differently to increase its odds of getting to done by the end of the sprint, as shown in the figure on page 153.

Here's how you can help your team members collaborate and make sure they're ready to tackle the next day of their sprint:

- Focus on the work. Use your team board to guide the conversation. For each product backlog item, discuss blockers, progress, and the tasks the

team will work on today. Seek insights from multiple team members. Doing so will give everyone a shared understanding of what work is in process, where the dependencies are, and how any risks will be mitigated.

- Keep the team board up to date. There are people in your organization who want true status reports. By encouraging the development team to keep their board current, you help create a tool that can provide valuable information to others. Management can walk by the board and see at a glance how things are progressing. This transparency into the work is a great way to build trust with stakeholders.

- Boot the peanut gallery. If someone outside the development team is overpowering the daily scrum, ask them to leave and have a member of the development team facilitate the discussion. You'd be surprised what a new voice can help bring to light. If the problem is *you*, then either force yourself to remain silent or simply don't attend. (We talk more about this in the next section.)

- Keep the development team's eyes on the sprint goal. The purpose of the sprint goal is to remind the team why they're building the current increment of software. As new work, ideas, or decisions come up in the daily scrum, use the sprint goal as your guidepost to filter out the noise and keep the team focused on the high-priority work.

The daily scrum is meant to communicate so much more than just status updates. Try these techniques and see if they help improve your team's daily scrum.

All Eyes on the Scrum Master

As we've mentioned, the Scrum master isn't the focal point of the daily scrum. In fact, they don't even have to attend the event. But if your daily scrum has turned into a status meeting, you might find yourself at the center of the event. If you notice that the development team is talking to you and not to each other, it's time to make an adjustment.

Take a step back from the group to emphasize that you're outside of the discussion. Turn away from the team and face the wall. Yes, it's silly, but the message is clear—the daily scrum is for the development team, not the Scrum master.

Remove yourself from the center of the conversation and enable the team to collaborate with each other. This will help put the focus back on the sprint goal and help the team to self-organize and create a new plan for the day. This is yet another reminder to you, the Scrum master, that very little about the role is about you. Welcome to servant leadership.

The Twice-a-Week Scrum

The daily scrum is a daily event. That statement sounds obvious—it's the *daily* scrum after all—but many Scrum teams want to hold it every other day or even less frequently.

Some team members might complain that not a lot changes day-to-day and that they'd rather have their 15 minutes back. Others may feel so much pressure to deliver as many features as possible that they'll claim they're too busy to attend yet another meeting.

When the team reacts this way, you can bet that there's pressure coming from somewhere. Maybe the pressure is self-inflicted. If the team overcommitted or put too much work on their sprint backlog, cutting meetings might sound appealing. Or maybe the pressure is coming from looming deadlines, or from stakeholders or management. Or perhaps other Scrum anti-patterns are to blame, and they're causing the development team to not get any value from the daily scrum.

Above all, remember that *the daily scrum is for the development team members.* This is their event, and they need it. Over the course of a two-week sprint, things can and do change rapidly. If the development team doesn't stop and inspect their progress frequently, they run the risk of missing opportunities to adapt their work in time to achieve the sprint goal. The daily scrum is an inflection point. It's a dynamic replanning session where the team takes into account progress, changes, impediments, and new insights from the entire team, and decides what to do next.

One possible solution to a development team not wanting to have a daily scrum every day is to facilitate a discussion about commitment. Start by reiterating the purpose of the daily scrum. Remind team members that part of their commitment is following the Scrum framework. Then ask team members for their input about what could happen if they don't meet daily to get aligned on their work. This is a great opportunity to explore what the team is experiencing, and see if they can find ways to solve the root problems.

If the team decides that that daily scrum isn't valuable, ask them what would need to change to *make* it valuable. Use these ideas to come up with experiments that the team can carry out to try to improve their daily scrum facilitation and practices.

Not All Voices Are Heard

On some Scrum teams, certain development team members do a lot of talking during the daily scrum, while others rarely say a word. Treating everyone with respect is a great way to resolve this problem. As the Scrum master, you should facilitate the daily scrum in a way that makes sure every voice is heard and that multiple viewpoints are considered. Especially when you're working with a new team, you need to model this listening and receptiveness to various viewpoints.

For instance, say you have a team member who dominates the daily scrum. If this happens frequently, ask the other team members for their viewpoints and hold the space—keep your mouth shut—until someone speaks. The silence will get uncomfortable, but eventually someone will provide some insights about the issue the team is discussing.

Or try using a talking stick or a beach ball: The team member who holds the item has the floor, and then they pass it along to the next team member when they're finished. Using a physical item to designate whose turn it is to talk can cut down on cross talk and side conversations. The focus stays on the work, and the team is respectful of the person speaking.

You can also consider using a liberating structure. For example, a good place to start is to try using a 1-2-4-All to facilitate your daily scrum so that all voices are heard. Here's how it works:

1. Ask the development team members to spend one minute silently considering the following question: "What opportunities do you see for making progress on the team's sprint goal?"

2. Next, have them spend two minutes working in pairs to generate ideas and build on their insights from the self-reflection they did in step 1.

3. Once they've explored these ideas in pairs, have the pairs form foursomes and spend four minutes sharing and developing these ideas even further, paying special attention to the similarities, differences, and patterns they notice during their discussion.

4. Finally, ask the team "What idea really stood out during your conversations?" Have each group share one idea with the entire Scrum team.

Notice how 1-2-4-All supports the Scrum value of openness. Each person has an opportunity to share their viewpoint and to have their voice heard while feeling safe sharing their ideas and the things they learned during the daily scrum.

Another technique you can try is Fist of Five voting, which is great way to get quick feedback about an idea during the daily scrum. Let's say that you ask your team if there are any impediments, but you don't get much feedback. You sense there must be a better way to gauge the mood of the team. This is a good opportunity to give Fist of Five voting a try. It's a facilitation technique that can help you measure the team's level of confidence in a value statement. (A value statement is the question or idea that you're getting feedback about.) The name comes from team members using their fingers to vote on a scale from 1 to 5:

Five Fingers: Yes! I'm 100% aligned with the value statement. Four Fingers: I strongly support the value statement. Three Fingers: I want to discuss the value statement before giving my support. Two Fingers: I oppose the value statement. One Finger: NO! Absolutely not! The value statement is wrong.

For example, during a daily scrum meeting, you might ask the team, "How confident are you that we're on track to meet the sprint goal?" Tell them to think about the question and come up with their answer on the scale of 1 to 5. Then have everyone show the number of fingers that represents their response.

Next, ask the 1s and 2s to talk about why their confidence is low. Ask them, "What's stopping you from voting higher?" After their initial discussion, the Scrum team members can vote again and see if they're more aligned than before.

This technique has several benefits:

- Low ceremony: It's very simple to do—all you need is a question and a fist. After that, it's up to the team members to discuss their scores and work toward alignment.

- Encourages participation: People who aren't involved aren't committed to the Scrum team. Fist of Five gets all team members involved in the conversation. The 1s and 2s get a nonconfrontational opportunity to express their concerns, allowing the team to learn together.

- Makes "no" easier: "No" is an incredibly hard word to say, especially when you have to say it to your teammates. Fist of Five allows Scrum team members the chance to disagree with the question being asked without being disagreeable. That's the key to creating open and honest conversations.

- Creates alignment: An aligned team is a powerful team. The goal of the vote is to get the team to collaborate and converge on an agreed-upon number. Taking the time to address the 1s and 2s gets everyone involved.

- Leads to action: The alignment process tends to draw out the reasons why Scrum team members aren't confident. For example, perhaps the automated build isn't so automated, or maybe there's a major flaw in the architecture that makes the sprint goal difficult. Knowing these impediments gives the team a clear list of action items to work on.

Fist of Five is a technique that you can use any time you sense that the team lacks confidence. The status of the current sprint, the likelihood of achieving the sprint goal, or even the state of the sprint backlog are all great topics for it. Hopefully, you'll find that the numbers are really secondary to the rich conversations that your Scrum team engages in and the actions they ultimately take.

The Team Isn't Making Progress

When watching a development team conduct a daily scrum, you'll often notice tasks that are blocked—ones where the team isn't making any progress. Sometimes it seems like these tasks are glued to the team board: they just won't move. Even worse, the result of the daily scrum probably won't address the blocked tasks.

A development team is accountable for their progress, and an important part of that is pointing out and tackling blockers and impediments as a team as soon as possible. When tasks and stories appear stuck and no one is talking, it's time to get concerned about why the team isn't speaking up. If team members simply aren't aware that they can speak up, remind them that the whole point of the daily scrum is for them to discuss any impediments and, as a team, make a plan to overcome them.

Another possibility is that the team has so much work in progress that they simply haven't noticed the stuck task. To make this issue more visible, consider tracking work item aging: the amount of time that has elapsed since the team started on a work item. It's easy! At the end of each day, simply take a marker and put a dot on every in-progress card. If the card doesn't move to a new status on the board, add another dot the next day. During the daily scrum, ask the development team to focus on the oldest cards (those with the most dots). Use this data to start a conversation with the development team about how to get the task moving again. Even better, use this as an opportunity to talk about the value of limiting the amount of work in progress. For example, when the next daily scrum is over and the team is still around the team board, ask them how their plan for the day addresses the stuck PBIs. This gentle nudge could be enough to make the point that we, as a team, are accountable for achieving the sprint goal and that we're committed to helping each other when needed.

Keep in mind that a team member (or members) may not feel comfortable speaking up in the daily scrum. When a task or story is stuck and the person doing the work isn't asking for help, you can bet that the team isn't living the Scrum values. Try discussing the Scrum values with your team. Ask them which values are missing when team members stop offering and asking for help. Use this list of values to start the conversation:

- Commitment: The members of the development team are committed to following the rules of Scrum, and to helping one another deliver a high-quality increment of valuable software.

- Focus: The sprint goal creates focus for the development team. It's a guidepost that the team can use to make rapid decisions. For example, the team may have to decide whether to accept additional work during the sprint. If the new work puts the sprint goal in jeopardy, the answer is a clear no.

- Courage: It takes courage to raise an impediment to the team, to ask for help with a story that has you stumped, or to raise a concern about the direction the team is going. Development team members must show courage and act transparently for the betterment of the team, especially when they realize that they're wrong and need to pivot quickly to realign to the sprint goal.

- Openness: The team members need to be open with one another to keep their progress toward the sprint goal transparent. Otherwise, the team won't be able to inspect and adapt. Openness allows team members to both offer and ask for help. Openness also helps us listen to all voices and opinions so that the team has ownership of its decisions.

- Respect: The daily scrum is intense. All the work is out in the open so the team can inspect and adapt. Team members may need to ask for help or have differing opinions. Without respect for each other and for everyone's abilities, empiricism and self-organization just aren't possible.

Having honest conversations about the Scrum values and how the team may not be embodying them can be tough. Asking for help and offering help at the risk of insulting someone can feel uncomfortable. But if you're living the Scrum values, these things will become easier over time.

Punishing Tardiness

Some Scrum masters lock the door to the conference room once the daily scrum starts. It may seem like, by creating a consequence for being late, you're helping the team members show up on time. But punishments like closing the door, a late jar, and making people sing or dance if they're late are acts of pillory. Public shaming isn't one of the tools of a Scrum master.

Team members who don't respect each other enough to be on time to a team event are exposing a problem that can't be solved by doing a silly dance. You'll need to dig deeper and work with the team to discover what's going on.

For example, did the team get to decide when and where to hold the daily scrum? It's their event—let them choose how to conduct it.

Does the team have a sprint goal, or is the daily scrum just a status report? If these issues are present, you'll need to work through them to get the team to attend on time.

Sometimes people believe that the only work worth doing is sitting in front of a computer screen writing code. If you're making widgets, this could make sense. But we work in a complex domain and perform knowledge work. Most of the time and energy that goes into software development involves thinking. It's essential that the team collaborates frequently about where everyone expects to be the next day, because doing this creates a shared understanding that everyone can leverage.

This may feel inefficient to some members of the development team, but the outcomes the daily scrum produces—alignment, focus, commitment, and purpose—are essential to high-performing teams.

The 45-Minute Scrum

During any meeting, most people get fidgety at about the nine-minute mark. By the time the team hits the 15-minute time box for the daily scrum, they're ready to put the new plan into action. And this happens during *well-executed* daily scrum. If a daily scrum hits a whopping 45 minutes, your team has definitely checked out and is no longer paying attention. (It's a miracle if they're still awake.)

Some people think that if they just keep talking, they'll sound like they're giving an informed answer. These kind of rambling answers are a common cause of daily scrums lasting longer than the 15-minute limit. If your daily scrum is feeling like a *daily bore*, start listening a little harder. You'll often hear generic answers, overly technical answers, vague hand-waving about work getting done "soon," and other unprepared answers. You may also see the daily scrum get hijacked by people who are trying to solve problems, refine product backlog items, gather status reports from the Scrum team, perform a monolog, or are simply procrastinating. None of those activities should to be part of the daily scrum. The point is to quickly create a plan for making progress over the next 24 hours—that's it.

The time box for the daily scrum is 15 minutes. If your development team is taking longer than that to conduct the event, they have a serious focus problem.

So how do you go about fixing this? The first question to consider is: What's the hold up? Are there too many team members? Are teams trying to solve development issues during the daily scrum? Is the product owner using this time to provide details on product backlog items? Wait...why is the product owner participating in the daily scrum?

Once you have a handle on where the time is going, you can start to make some corrections. We've already discussed using a physical team board. This technique alone can bring focus back to your daily scrum.

If the team is going off on tangents or trying to solve problems, try using a parking lot: a list of things to possibly discuss *after* the daily scrum. Members of the development team can then decide how to clear the items off the parking lot (self-organization) and move on with their day.

If you don't have the sprint goal at the top of your team board already, now is a great time to post it up there. Any time the team goes off on a tangent, team members can point to the sprint goal as a reminder to stay on track. A great question to ask when the team goes off on a tangent during the daily scrum is, "How does this conversation contribute to our plan to make progress toward the sprint goal?"

Pointing to the sprint goal is a powerful gesture that can help restore focus to your daily scrum and turn these long bore-fests into valuable and productive planning sessions—that last 15 minutes or less.

The Team is Raising False Impediments

During a daily scrum with a development team where Ryan was serving as Scrum master, the team realized that some of the team members didn't have enough work to keep them busy until the end of the current sprint. They raised this situation as an impediment to Ryan, and wanted him to find them more work.

If your team makes a request like this, you might be tempted to work with the product owner to find more work for the team. But is not having enough work in the sprint really an impediment? Nope—it really isn't. If the team has extra time and can pull in work, they can do that on their own with some guidance from the product owner. The true impediment here is that the development team isn't collaborating around the remaining work so that everyone has an opportunity to contribute to achieving the sprint goal. (For a refresher on what qualifies as an impediment, flip back to What's an Impediment?, on page 151.) The development team is empowered to pull work into a sprint. The team owns the sprint backlog and decides how to do their work.

Sometimes the right answer to a development team raising an impediment is simply, "How fascinating! I can't wait to see how you tackle that issue."

Whenever a Scrum team raises an impediment, stop and ask yourself two questions:

1. Is this actually an impediment or is it a sign that the team doesn't understand self-organization yet?

2. If this really is an impediment, is it something the team can remove on its own?

Keep these questions in mind as you handle impediments. What looks like an impediment could actually be a wonderful opportunity for the development team to practice self-organization.

Coach's Corner

If your Daily Scrum doesn't suffer from any of the major anti-patterns we discussed in this chapter, but you still feel like it could be more productive, here are a few things that you can try during your next daily scrum:

1. At the beginning of your next daily scrum, take a few minutes to remind the team of its purpose.

2. Remove yourself from the circle of development team members to put focus on the sprint goal and to help avoid the daily scrum devolving to a status meeting.

3. If you need to participate during the daily scrum—especially with new teams—try to limit yourself to open-ended questions that promote transparency, encourage inspecting the sprint goal, and promote adaptation by creating a new plan for the day.

4. Skip attending the daily scrum every once in a while and see what happens. Hopefully, the development team will still hold the event, align on their work, and develop a plan for the day that helps them achieve the sprint goal.

5. If people other than development team members participate in the daily scrum, ask them to stop and practice their active listening skills. The daily scrum *is for the development team.*

6. Coach the development team to own the daily scrum by setting the time, setting the place, and deciding how best to measure their progress toward the sprint goal. Remind the development team that they own the team board, the sprint backlog, and how they monitor their progress. Encourage them to keep their progress transparent.

7. Remind your team to be open to receiving help. We all get stuck. Don't stay stuck. Be courageous. Their teammates are there to help each other.

In the next chapter, we'll take a look at the done product increment. Delivering an increment of product is why we're all here—it's the purpose of Scrum. But if you ask most Scrum team members what a done increment is, they struggle. We'll help clear up this confusion so your team can be confident that they're on the right track.

CHAPTER 13

Deconstructing the Done Product Increment

It's super important that everyone on a Scrum team knows what constitutes "done" for a specific project. Otherwise, you'll end up having conversations like this:

> *Product Owner: Hey, I'm just checking in on the new shopping cart for our site. I had a customer ask about it, so I thought I'd see if it's available for a quick demo.*
>
> *Development Team: Of course, the shopping cart is done.*
>
> *Product Owner: It's done? That's great. Let's go ahead and deploy it early. This could really help on the next sales calls. Great job everyone!*
>
> *Development Team: Well wait...we can't deploy it. We don't have the build scripts ready and the database changes are still being worked on, plus the unit tests aren't complete yet...*
>
> *Product Owner: You just said it was done.*
>
> *Development Team: Well yeah, the shopping cart works locally—mostly. But it isn't done-done.*
>
> *Product Owner: Done-done?*
>
> *Development Team: Yeah, that's when we can ship it. Right now it's just done.*

And with that, the product owner and development team go their separate ways. Best case: both sides are equally confused about what just happened. Worst case: the product owner will never again trust the development team when they say that something is "done."

Many teams struggle to create a done product increment by the end of each sprint. (An increment is the sum of all PBIs that were completed in the sprint, along with the sum of all product increments that were created in previous sprints.) They write code and they test it, but there are a lot of branches in the code repository that need to be merged. Then new code must be integrated and tested with previous increments, but all of that work seems daunting to accomplish in a single sprint while trying to add new features.

There are lots of reasons why teams end up in this situation:

- New teams members join

- Others leave the company

- Developers are assigned to multiple projects

- There's no sprint goal

- Sprint planning is poor

- There were no refinement sessions during the sprint

- Product backlog items are either too big or unclear

- The product owner is absent

- Impediments are piling up

- Technical debt is slowing the team

- The development team doesn't have all skills it needs to deliver a done increment

- Team members aren't working together

In other words, all the Scrum anti-patterns in this book can—and often do—lead to a Scrum team that doesn't have a done product increment at the end of the sprint.

It's also possible that your team is new to Scrum and everyone is learning how to work in a new way. Learning is part of the game of Scrum. Sometimes the team has to fail in order to learn to deliver high-quality software. Failures give team members an opportunity to learn why they didn't get to done during the current sprint, and they can make changes that will help them improve during the next sprint.

The sprint retrospective is a great time to explore these opportunities to improve. As your team comes up with issues that prevented them from releasing a done product increment, refer to the appropriate chapter in this book to find some ideas of things to try next.

> \|//
> ꭚ   **Joe asks:**
> # Our increment isn't releasable. Are we doing Scrum?
>
> This type of question is what we in the training community call a Scrum Grenade. Often, the best answer to this question is a sly grin followed by "It depends." Honestly, it doesn't really matter: If you and your team are working toward adopting Scrum and are improving every sprint, don't worry about whether someone thinks you're doing Scrum. Just focus on creating working, releasable software as soon as responsibly possible.

Your Scrum team needs to have available a tested, integrated, deployable, and usable version of your product at all times. The goal is to improve the increment every few days while keeping it in a ready-to-use—and potentially releasable—state. If the product owner wants to release the latest increment at a moment's notice, that should be a low-risk and simple task.

Yes, this sets the bar high, but keep in mind that the development team creates and owns the definition of "done." Having a done product increment every sprint is one of the central tasks required of a development team, so by using Scrum, the development team has committed to creating quality products and delivering done increments. The team is also focused on delivery and service to the product owner.

A good definition of done is transparent—it allows everyone on the Scrum team to know when an increment is done. It's also specific to the development team's situation and the skills that they have, which is why it's created and owned by the dev team. If the development team falls under an overarching software development department or product development area, a definition of done may be created at that level. But then, each development team inherits it and makes it more strict to fit their situation and abilities.

The definition of done should be a list of qualities that describe the completeness of a product increment. For example, the definition of done could include "training materials completed for all features." That way, when you tell the product owner and stakeholders that the increment is done, they'll know that they're looking at features that include the documentation the customer needs. By being open with the product owner and stakeholders, the development team can discuss improvement opportunities openly and work collaboratively to get better results in the next sprint.

Throughout this chapter, we'll explore what "done" means, how your team can build a useful definition of done, and the characteristics of a product increment. As you'll see, not having a shared understanding of done can cause all sorts of headaches. We'll help you avoid these problems or, if you're *already* dealing with them, suggest ways to improve your current situation.

We Haven't Defined "Done"

Many teams struggle to create a definition of done. Without such a definition, the team loses transparency into the product increment, and all sorts of problems can arise:

- The product owner won't understand the level of completeness of each feature or how much time the team needs to release the features to customers.

- The development team will struggle to measure its velocity or progress within a sprint due to increasing technical debt and an incomplete understanding of what "done" means.

- The product backlog is likely incomplete because the Scrum team isn't sharing and frequently reviewing testing requirements, nonfunctional requirements, and organizational standards.

- The development team won't know how many product backlog items to select during sprint planning. Product backlog items that seem simple could cause big problems that remain hidden until late in the sprint. Testing and integrations can significantly increase complexity.

- The stakeholders won't understand what could potentially be released to customers.

These are just a few examples of how a Scrum team can lose transparency without a shared understanding of what done means. Without transparency, inspection and adaptation mean nothing. When the Scrum team isn't working toward done, they lose sight of the Scrum values.

Here's a format that many teams use to facilitate creating a definition of done. You'll need a whiteboard, sticky notes, and markers. Follow these steps to give your team a great starting point that they can use, learn from, and improve over time.

1. Consider when certain tasks need to be done. For example, it might make sense to list tasks that are completed at the product backlog item, sprint, and release levels. Decide as a team which categories make sense for you.

2. Using your categories from step 1, create areas on the whiteboard where your team can brainstorm tasks that fit into each category.

3. Give each team member a stack of sticky notes and a marker. Ask them to spend five minutes writing down as many tasks as they can think of for each category. At the end of the five minutes, ask each person to place their sticky note in the space designated for each category.

4. Work with the team to eliminate duplicates and to clarify what each note means. Consider giving team members a chance to move sticky notes and create new ones. This can help keep everyone engaged and interested in the discussion.

5. Make sure the team is considering more than just coding activities. (Your product owner can help with this.) For example, did the team consider business issues? Are service-level agreements in place? What about company standards and policies? Considering these aspects helps ensure that you have a holistic definition of done.

6. Once you have consensus and a shared understanding about each sticky note, ask the Scrum team to walk around the room and put a dot on any of the sticky notes that they believe will be difficult or even impossible to finish during a sprint. Remind the team that all the items they place in the definition of "done" must be completed by the conclusion of each sprint. If that's not a possibility, then remove items to create a less strict definition of "done."

7. Discuss the sticky notes that accumulated the most dots and find ways to compromise on those tasks without sacrificing overall quality. You'll likely discover many possible process and development improvements the Scrum team will need to address over the next few sprints.

8. Decide which sticky notes will survive and become part of your Definition of "done."

This is the team's first crack at creating such a definition. But this definition can—and should—change over time. Your team should regularly inspect its definition of done during sprint retrospectives. How often it makes sense to do this depends on your specific circumstances.

So what does a definition of "done" look like? Here's an example:

- All code has been developed.

- It meets the team's coding standards.

- Unit tests are written and passing.

- Code has been checked into the source control repository.

- Acceptance criteria have been met and confirmed by a development team member who didn't write the code.

- The continuous integration build is passing.

- The product owner has seen the product (increment).

- All code has been deployed to the staging environment.

The preceding example is from a development team that Todd worked with that strived to always have an increment that was in a releasable state. This team could release features to production whenever the product owner needed new features to go live. When the development team said they were "done," it was clear to the product owner what state the completed work was in. Having the code always in a releasable state gave the product owner a lot of flexibility in choosing when to release. In many organizations, there are many impediments that must be removed before teams can release products on demand. As the Scrum master, it's your job to abolish those impediments.

As we mentioned, this is just an example. Use it. Modify it. Better yet, brainstorm with your team to create your own definition of done! Scrum requires that every increment be releasable, so work with your team to create a definition of done that makes that possible.

"But you said it was done…"
by: Todd Miller

I was an Agile coach in an organization that needed help scaling Scrum. There were four development teams, a Scrum master for each, and one product owner who worked with all four teams. I observed an interesting interaction between a development team member and the product owner: The developer said they were "done" with a feature, and the product owner got really excited about playing with the new functionality in the test environment. Looking nervous, the developer admitted that he had just finished writing the code and that it would be several days until the product owner could actually use the feature.

I started asking questions and came to find that none of the development teams nor the software development organization as a whole had a definition of done. In fact, not only was there often confusion with what a team meant when they said they were "done," but individuals within the teams weren't sure either.

Along with the Scrum masters, I helped the development teams agree on a simple, common definition of "done." This alone created a remarkable amount of transparency. There was a sharp decrease in the number of production bugs reported, the development teams and product owner had clear expectations of each other, and the teams were able to focus on quality.

Being contextual, the definition of done changes along the way. See how things go. During your next sprint retrospective, you'll have the opportunity to inspect how things went and adapt your definition of done, if needed.

Cutting Quality to Hit a Release Date

Imagine that your Scrum team just got out of a heated sprint review. The team didn't deliver anything during this sprint, and the stakeholders are furious. Deadlines were reiterated and ultimatums delivered: "You will deliver everything in this next sprint or else!"

Then temptation creeps in: What if you removed the requirement to write unit tests during the sprint? You could just add them later when you aren't under so much pressure.

The truth is there will never be a time when your team isn't under pressure. And once you start down the path of sacrificing quality to meet dates, you'll find that your productivity steadily declines over time as your technical debt increases.

In these situations, Scrum masters really earn their keep. Here's an important question you should ask the development team and the product owner: Does removing a requirement from the definition of done uphold our commitment to quality and allow the team to deliver a potentially shippable increment by the end of the sprint?" If the answer is a resoundingYes," then great! You've found a constraint that you can likely remove without much impact. But when the answer is "No," it's time to look elsewhere for solutions.

Why? Because undone work—work that the development team *claims* is done, but for which there is still more work remaining—is never part of the increment.

For example, suppose a development team says they are done creating a new shipping feature for a website that will allow real-time shipping quotes to customers via USPS. Though they say it's done, it hasn't been tested to confirm that it works with the organization's shipping and receiving system because they can only mock the system, not test in a fully integrated environment. So while they're done with the feature in their development environment, testing the integration with the shipping and receiving system is undone work because it's not completed yet.

Undone work should never be put into production–*ever*. In our example scenario, if the team puts the undone work into production there could be dire consequences to the organization's shipping and receiving system. As Scrum masters, we must take the impediment (in this case, the team's inability to do full integration testing against the shipping and receiving system) into our hands and work within the organization to remove it.

Joe asks:
Why can't we release undone work?

Each increment gets added to all prior increments and thoroughly tested, ensuring that all increments work together. This rule comes straight from The Scrum Guide. Undone work doesn't meet that criteria, so it can never, ever be released.

Consider what would happen if you made an exception to this rule. How would you know the impact your software has on your customers if you neglected quality and allowed undone work into production? You wouldn't—until it's too late and customers are reporting a degradation of quality in your product. The short-sighted decision to release undone work increases your team's risk of failure. It will become a habit, quality will degrade, and your customers will notice. It simply isn't worth the risk.

A done product increment is usable. If you release it, it doesn't break in production. There are no bugs, no glitches, no half-baked features. A released product increment that the team calls done is valuable, it's of high quality, and it works as intended when the customer uses it.

When balancing quality and deadlines, try mapping out your last sprint on a whiteboard or with sticky notes and markers. Start at the end with the increment and work backward. Put your Scrum events on the wall and include any major events from the sprint. Did your team composition change? Did you get new product backlog items mid-sprint? How did refinement go? Was the daily scrum productive and focused on the sprint goal? (You had a sprint goal, right?) Use the insights you gain from this discussion to come up with improvements that will allow you to deliver a done increment.

If you're under a deadline, revisit your product backlog items with your product owner. Work diligently with them to try to understand what is actually necessary and possible. Working with the team, you may try to find ways to slice your PBIs into smaller pieces that are still valuable and shippable within a sprint.

Approaching a deadline by negotiating scope and/or decomposing PBIs into smaller chunks changes the discussion in an important way. Rather than trying to negotiate an estimate or a date, you're negotiating scope. Cutting the features that aren't truly needed by the deadline and slicing the features that are needed can help a team make progress under stressful conditions while preserving quality.

We'll Finish That Later

You have a done product increment that you could potentially release, but it requires some manual intervention to release it into production. The remaining undone work will perhaps take another day or two or three to complete.

This situation often leads to teams doing the remaining work at the end of the sprint or creating a sprint specifically for completing that work. When that happens, feedback loops and cycles get way too large. You can't release this untested, unchecked software to production. Without a release, you aren't getting feedback, which means you can't validate the value of your product. Similarly, the further you move away from the partially completed work, the harder it is to switch contexts, hop back into the work, and finish it.

This distance between "done" and released to customers is a measure of agility. The greater the distance, the lower your ability to respond to opportunities in the market and to changing conditions that you could capitalize on. The greater this distance is, the higher your overall risk.

Some teams address this with specialized sprints that focus on a particular aspect of product development such as testing, requirements gathering, or designing. But specialized sprints aren't a part of Scrum. We dive deep into these anti-patterns in Chapter 9, Thinking in Sprints, on page 105.

A common specialized sprint is the hardening sprint, where Scrum teams work on things like integration testing, performance tuning, security reviews, and localization. Often, this type of sprint becomes a catch-all for new features, sloppy code, bug fixes, and other work that signals poor craftsmanship. Hardening sprints, simply put, are an excuse to delay quality and we recommend *never* using them. Be on alert for these reasons teams often give for wanting a hardening sprint:

- We ran out of time and didn't fully test this feature. We'll finish testing during the hardening sprint.

- User documentation didn't quite get done for this feature. I'll finish that up during the hardening sprint.

- No need to engage support or security or infrastructure now—we'll bring them up to speed during the hardening sprint.

- We'll wait to write unit tests for this during the hardening sprint.

If you're currently using a hardening sprint, it's time to stop and address the reasons why the team can't build a potentially releasable increment by the end of a sprint. Teams that are new to Scrum often don't have all the practices and processes in place that they need to release to production in a repeatable and reliable way. And that's okay. However, these are impediments that a development team needs to address.

Continuous integration, test automation, and strong DevOps practices take time to build and implement, along with a lot of money and often new skill sets. If you're in the early stages of a Scrum adoption, your team may find hardening sprints tempting because you might not have some or all of these practices in place. Resist the urge to use hardening sprints and instead take productive steps toward improving your practices to achieve "done" by the end of a sprint.

Coach's Corner

Do you have a definition of done that your whole Scrum team and their stakeholders understand? If not, use the exercise we discussed in this chapter to get your first definition captured and posted for everyone to see.

If you *do* have a definition of done, when was the last time you reviewed it during your sprint retrospective? Whether it's been one sprint or ten since you've inspected and adapted your definition of done, use your next retrospective to start a conversation around the development team's commitment to quality, and use that time to make sure the current definition of done supports that commitment.

As the Scrum master, you'll need to do a lot of facilitating during this discussion. The team will have limiting beliefs about what they're capable of doing. They'll have even deeper beliefs about what they're allowed to do. Openness and respect are crucial to this conversation. There might be development practices you need to implement, like continuous integration, continuous delivery, test-driven development, and automated testing.

The development team members own how they do their work. The definition of done reflects that ownership. During the next sprint review meeting, take some time to present the definition of done to your stakeholders. Show them that quality is important. This could make future trade-off discussions go more smoothly.

If there are impediments to delivering a high-quality product increment that the team can't solve on its own, raise those issues to management right away.

You'll want to get an impediment list going, and plan out how to get those impediments resolved as quickly as possible.

In this chapter, we explored the importance of developing potentially shippable "done" increments. In the next chapter, we'll discuss the sprint review, where the Scrum team meets with the product stakeholders to inspect the product increment and discuss budgets, forecasts, release, and updates that could impact the vision and direction of the product. The importance of the definition of done and the transparency it brings will be front and center in this discussion.

CHAPTER 14

The Sprint Review

It's really common for Scrum teams to misuse sprint reviews and have the event go off the rails—we see it all the time in our consulting. Here's a situation Todd witnessed that illustrates some of the many ways that sprint reviews can fail.

A few years ago, Todd was asked to consult with a product owner at a non-profit company. The company had an old-school, manual process for issuing donation receipts to donors that involved paper, pens, and the postal system. They dreamed of a digital system that would free up employee time so that employees could focus their energy on other, more important tasks like inciting donors to keep giving to their cause. The nonprofit's board passed a budget and anointed as product owner a manager with in-depth knowledge of the donation processes. The remainder of the Scrum team was assembled, and off they went on their first sprint to begin fulfilling the company's digital donation receipt dream.

The first sprint began with the product owner telling the team her expectations of what they were going to complete during the sprint. At the first sprint review, the Scrum team gathered, and the product owner carefully inspected the work the development team had completed during that sprint. The development team went through each PBI in the sprint backlog as the product owner gave a thumbs up or down to signify whether she accepted or rejected the work. The product owner made it clear that she wasn't terribly upset with the results because it was the team's first sprint, but that there was certainly room for improvement.

A few sprints into the project, the development team started sensing a disconnect between the product owner and some of the stakeholders with which the development team had been discussing scope. Todd made a visit to the organization and suggested to the product owner that she might want to invite some stakeholders to the next sprint review. The product owner scoffed and said that she knew what was best for the department and that all of the stakeholders' opinions would add unnecessary scope.

After several months, nothing had shipped, and pressure began to mount on the product owner. The organization was ailing from all of the manual work. When the pressure became too great, the product owner finally took Todd's advice and invited stakeholders to the sprint review, including some back-end office employees and a few executives who had approved the project's funding. As the development team demonstrated their working software, the frustrated stakeholders raised lots of questions:

- "Have you considered what will happen with foreign currencies?"

- "How will this integrate with our customer relationship management system?"

- "Will the receipts be available on a mobile device?"

- "Did you handle these edge cases?"

The stakeholders were surprised that the software wasn't even close to being ready for production. The people who had funded the effort were especially upset: They argued that many of the issues identified in the sprint review should have been raised very early in discussions. They remarked that Scrum doesn't work, and that with a better upfront plan, these items would have been considered during the requirements phase. A few days later the project was canceled, the product owner was fired, and the Scrum team disbanded.

The product owner in this example refused to invite stakeholders to the sprint review out of fear that the project's scope might expand beyond of her control. She treated the review as a mechanism for her to accept or reject the team's work—not as an opportunity to get feedback from stakeholders. The lack of transparency to the wider organization outside of the Scrum team caused the company to waste a lot of money, and not solve the problem that the project was meant to fix.

The sprint review is an important event that occurs toward the end of a sprint. It's where the Scrum team inspects the increment and adapts the product backlog. In collaboration with stakeholders, the Scrum team reviews what has happened and decides what to do next. There are many problems that can arise from noncollaborative sprint reviews. Let's explore some of these anti-patterns—and how to avoid them.

Stakeholders Aren't Involved

In the nonprofit example we just described, excluding stakeholders from the sprint review was the key point of failure for the project. Your product owner may *want* to delay conversations about your project's scope and about stakeholders' wants and needs, but that's not the right thing to do. As you just saw, such lack of transparency can kill a product.

 Joe asks:

Who are my stakeholders?

A stakeholder is anyone who has a vested interest in the outcome of a product-development effort. From employees whose jobs will be changed by the project to the folks who approved funding for it, stakeholders can come from all corners of an organization. Who they are depends on the nature of the product.

A product owner should understand who their stakeholders are and have searched every corner of the organization to ensure that they have appropriately defined and included everyone. Also, keep in mind that the stakeholders may change throughout the life cycle of the development effort. The product owner should occasionally revisit their list of stakeholders and check to see whether anyone should be added to or removed from that list.

Product owners must know who the stakeholders are at any given moment. They need to make sure that the appropriate people are involved in the sprint review so that the increment is properly inspected. As the Scrum master, work with your product owner to ensure that they have identified stakeholders from every corner of your organization. Product owners should be just as wary about having *not enough* stakeholder representation in the room during sprint reviews as they are of having too much.

An important component of Scrum, and one that impacts all the practices and principles of it, is building trust between the organization and the Scrum team. Having stakeholders attend sprint reviews helps build that trust, especially early in a product-development effort. Stakeholders need to actively participate in sprint reviews in order to understand what's happening with the product. This process leads to the product owner adapting the product backlog by incorporating new requirements, changes in the market, new mandates, and so on. Without the appropriate representation in a review, a Scrum team might be moving in the wrong direction.

If your product owner is having trouble identifying stakeholders, try this exercise:

1. Sit with your product owner—and perhaps some of the stakeholders they've already identified—and try to think of every person in the organization who has a vested interest in the outcome of what you're building. Write each person's name on a separate sticky note. If you get stuck, consider these questions:

    • Where is the money coming from?

    • Whose job is going to change because of this product?

    • Who might interact differently with a customer as a result of what we are building?

    • Who might be angry if they don't know what's going on with this project?

2. Once your brainstorming slows, take a break.

3. When you reconvene, create the following three categories on a whiteboard or flip chart, and then place each sticky note in the appropriate category:

    • Required for the Sprint Review: These are people who need the most information about the product. If these people don't inspect the increment and provide feedback, the Scrum team can't make informed changes to the product backlog.

    • Keep Informed of Progress: These are folks who don't need to inspect the increment every sprint, but who do need to be kept apprised of the team's progress.

    • Monitor: These are people who don't need updates frequently, but who should periodically receive updates about the project. It's best to check with them to see how often they'd like to receive these updates.

This exercise can give the product owner a good sense of where he should be spending his time. It's best to perform this activity every so often, since you might change which category you assign a stakeholder to over the course of a project.

The Product Owner as Judge

Here's a scenario we've seen many times and one that, as you may recall, occurred in the nonprofit example at the beginning of this chapter:

To prepare for each sprint review, the Scrum master and development team create an agenda to explain to the product owner what the team accomplished during the sprint. During the sprint review, the development team goes through each item, and the product owner approves or rejects the items for completeness. Regardless of whether any stakeholders are present, this process of acceptance or rejection is often the cause of much strife and angst for the development team.

The sprint review isn't an event where the product owner is supposed to act like a judge with a gavel. This behavior is a symptom of a lack of communication between the development team and product owner, and it breeds contempt within the dev team. If you see this anti-pattern developing, it's time to find ways to improve communication.

The development team and product owner should communicate throughout sprints so that the dev team's work is transparent and the PO is available to provide clarity around the PBIs in the current sprint. Without this kind of dialog, the product owner may end up being surprised during a sprint review, and the stakeholders may be equally if not more surprised. The product owner may in turn not be able to answer tough questions from stakeholders about the direction of the project or what the purpose of the last sprint was. This can lead to the development team having to do massive amounts of rework, which is frustrating for everyone.

Product owners typically have a lot of clout, so development teams may be intimidated and unsure of how to request better communication. This issue can be exacerbated if the product owner disappears after sprint planning—the dev team may interpret this as the product owner being haughty and unapproachable, though in all likelihood the PO is probably just busy and may simply not realize how important it is to be available to the dev team throughout every sprint.

Appropriate product owner-development team communication prevents rework, creates transparency, and heightens the chance of a development team completing the sprint goal. To encourage such collaboration, during sprint retrospectives, ask both the development team and the product owner whether they feel like their level of collaboration is appropriate to prevent misunderstandings between them. This will give them an opportunity to discuss ways to improve how they communicate with each other.

If you hear dev team members expressing frustration about the PO not being available, encourage the dev team to bring this up with the product owner so they're aware of it. Conversely, if you notice that the PO is surprised by some of the things the dev team brings up during the sprint review, work with the dev team to make sure they're keeping the product owner apprised of the team's progress throughout each sprint. You don't want frustrations like these to fester and cause rifts in your Scrum team. Your job is to foster a positive relationship between the development team and the product owner. Scrum cannot work well if these two roles cannot effectively collaborate. Frequent communication keeps everyone happy and on the same page.

Presenting Undone Work

Imagine there are three days left in the sprint, and stakeholder expectations are very high for the increment that the development team is building. Issues have emerged during the sprint that have slowed the development team, but the whole Scrum team has collaborated to keep the sprint goal intact. It's clear that, although the team will meet the sprint goal, some of the functionality the stakeholders were really excited about won't be fully tested and integrated into all environments. The development team's definition of done states that the code must be tested and integrated in order for it to be considered "done." But given the pressure from stakeholders, the Scrum team decides to include the functionality in the sprint review anyway.

During the sprint review, the team presents the untested/unintegrated work to the stakeholders. Despite the team trying to make it clear that the work isn't yet ready for production, stakeholders leave the meeting excited to have the functionality. A release happens the following day (as authorized by the product owner) but the untested/unintegrated features aren't part of it. The team plans to include those features in the next release.

After the release, stakeholders are disappointed because they expected to see more features than they got. They ask the product owner why features they saw the previous day aren't included. They don't understand what testing and integration means, but they think it sounds simple enough.

Presenting undone work in a sprint review leads to ill-informed stakeholders. Stakeholders are often outside of the Scrum bubble and don't fully comprehend the terminology that Scrum teams use. If, during a sprint review, stakeholders are disappointed by the team's lack of progress, a great opportunity exists to have a discussion about all the complex factors that affect the Scrum team and explain the issues that the team faced. Many product owners love the sprint review precisely because it gives them a chance to show stakeholders how hard and complicated the Scrum team's work is.

Joe asks:

Does it ever make sense to release undone software into production?

No. When the product increment isn't done by the end of a sprint, it's not potentially releasable. In Scrum, an increment is usable, tested, integrated with previous increments, and safe for a customer or stakeholder to use. If the increment isn't done, you don't know whether any of these criteria are true. It's too risky to release undone work because you can't know the impact (positive or negative) that using the untested product could have. When a development team doesn't meet the definition of done, they take away the product owner's ability to release to production.

Scrum teams should always be forthright about where things stand and not try to overstate their progress in order to please others. This is where you, the Scrum master, can really help the Scrum team understand that it's always better to be honest with stakeholders than to paint a rosy picture that isn't accurate.

Avoid the temptation to present undone work in a sprint review, or you may set false expectations. Presenting undone work to make it sound like the team has accomplished more than they really have isn't worth potentially degrading stakeholders' trust in the team. It's cliché, but honesty really *is* the best policy. If the team ran into problems during the sprint, be upfront about it and work with stakeholders to try to remove any impediments.

Treating Sprint Reviews like Demos

Here is another common scenario we see frequently: On the last day of the sprint, stakeholders meet with the Scrum team. The development team demos what they've accomplished since the last sprint review. The stakeholders inspect the new functionality and the product owner collects their feedback. After the review, the PO adapts the product backlog based on this feedback. Nobody—not stakeholders nor members of the Scrum team—has a clear understanding of the direction of the project. The stakeholders simply saw a demo but weren't given any context about how the team arrived at that increment.

In this scenario, the Scrum team was trying to do the right thing by meeting with stakeholders and allowing them to inspect the current increment, but they didn't present their progress in a way that was truly useful to the stakeholders. Stakeholders should know the reasoning behind the sprint goal that the team accomplished as well as the direction the project is headed.

Increment inspection should involve more than just demoing the functionality that the team has built since the last sprint review.

In order for the Scrum team to receive valuable feedback that can help them adapt the product backlog in an informed way and ensure that everyone (stakeholders and team members) truly understands the direction of the project, the team needs to create more transparency in sprint reviews. For example, here's an agenda that can help make the sprint review a truly collaborative session:

- Explanation of the product owner's vision for the product
- Review of the release plan and budget
- Description of the sprint goal for this sprint
- Review of the work and the product increment that the team built
- Assessment of current customer analytics and data
- Discussion of impediments the team is currently facing
- Collaboration with stakeholders to refine the product backlog
- Summary of where we're going next and what we discovered in this event

With this agenda, the whole Scrum team needs to be prepared to present during the meeting, so they can provide a holistic view of what has happened since the last sprint review and what might happen in the future. It's important that this event is viewed by both the Scrum team and stakeholders as a collaborative working session. The Scrum team must explain where they are, how they got there, what stands in their way, and where they're going. Simply giving a demo to stakeholders misses an opportunity to discuss broader topics around the project, and doesn't provide the product owner with fully informed stakeholder feedback for adapting the product backlog.

If your sprint reviews have become nothing more than demos, talk to your dev team and product owner about how you can make the event more collaborative (including using something similar to the sample agenda we provided). Doing so will make it a more worthwhile event for everyone involved, as shown in the figure on page 183.

There's an 'I' in Team

This is another scenario that we see quite a bit: During the sprint review, each developer takes a turn showing what he or she individually worked on during the sprint. The stakeholders are drawn to the more extroverted developers and view them as the heroes of the team. The more introverted developers have trouble explaining their work and speak quickly so they can "get off the stage."

Joe asks:
When should a team prepare for a sprint review?

The Scrum Guide doesn't answer this question, but there are many ways that teams can prepare for a sprint review. Ideally, the sprint review agenda emerges throughout the sprint. Your team may decide to have a short meeting prior to the sprint review to dot the i's and cross the t's. The product owner may want to massage the agenda, since they know the stakeholders well. And you, the Scrum master, can suggest new ways to facilitate the event so it's as collaborative as possible. However your team decides to craft the agenda, it's important that you do *some* preparation to make the event organized and productive.

Hearing the word "I" during a sprint review is a sign that there's dysfunction in the development team's self-organizing abilities, and that the team is operating as a collection of individuals rather than as a true team. Such dev teams are likely to start the sprint by individually claiming pieces of work. Then team members go off and work independently on their individual pieces. Seldom do these types of dev teams work on PBIs together, collectively trying to solve a problem.

The "I" mentality creates heroes on teams and gives stakeholders the illusion that one team member is contributing more than others. This gives stakeholders the wrong idea about a self-organizing development team's collective ownership of an increment: They see siloed developers accountable for individual features. Stakeholders will lay responsibilities for specific tasks on individual dev team members rather than the Scrum team as a whole. Blame over failures and joy over successes go to individuals instead of the whole Scrum team.

As we've discussed, the development team as a *whole* is accountable for the increment, not any individual team member. It takes a "we" mentality to create collective ownership. Teams fail to be self-organizing when they don't work together on PBIs. If each team member is only thinking about himself, then the team can't effectively work together to achieve the sprint goal.

> **Joe asks:**
> ## Who should talk during a sprint review?
>
> Everyone on the Scrum team should have the opportunity to speak in order to ensure that there's sufficient representation of every Scrum role. It's important that the people doing the work have the opportunity to present it. As a Scrum master, this can be a great opportunity for you to mentor and coach team members who are uncomfortable speaking in front of an audience.

There are many things a development team can do to help foster cooperation and collaboration among team members. Here are a few you may try:

- Limit the WIP (work in progress) of sprint backlog items during a sprint.

- Ensure that team members have a clear and concise sprint goal to self-organize around.

- Try pair programming.

- Experiment with mob programming, a technique where the whole team works on the same thing at the same time.

- Ban the word "I" on the team.

These techniques can really help your Scrum team remember to work *as a team*, which is what Scrum is all about. If you've been hearing a lot of I's during your sprint review, try some of these methods for getting everyone to refocus on what the whole team can accomplish—together.

The Stagnant Sprint Review

In this anti-pattern, stakeholders arrive at the sprint review with a clear expectation of what will occur, as the agenda has been the same for several sprints. Some stakeholders check email or work on their laptops until the team discusses something that's interesting to them, others funnel into the room late based on when they think the team will discuss information pertinent to them, and still others stop attending altogether. The stakeholders call the event "boring." None of the stakeholders seem to express their opinions unless something extraordinary piques their interest. The stakeholders and Scrum team feel that the project is no longer very risky since the project has been in-flight for several sprints. But that belief of less risk could very well be an illusion.

So how do you avoid this situation? First and foremost, the sprint review agenda should change to reflect the Scrum team's current circumstances, which shift frequently. (Stakeholders may change, too.) Varying the sprint review agenda is better than keeping it the same. A product owner should facilitate the sprint review in an engaging, collaborative way that involves everyone in attendance.

As Scrum master, you must work with your product owner and teach them how to lead the discussion to get the most out of the sprint review. If stakeholders are bored or uninterested, their lack of engagement will lead to missed opinions or ideas. The project can then be at risk because the team hasn't received the feedback it needs to make decisions. Customers may find issues with the product in production, and they may discover that the product is missing important features. Collaborative sprint reviews mean that the Scrum team gets ideas and suggestions from stakeholders so that the team can change the direction of the product, and stakeholders are able to raise any issues early on.

Frequently change the format of the sprint review to keep everyone on their toes. Try different kinds of facilitation techniques, such as ones that involve visualization or Liberating Structures.[1] Keep an eye out for participants who are quiet and get them involved in a nonintrusive, collaborative way. Do your best to solicit opinions from everyone in attendance so that no one's thoughts go unheard. Experiment with facilitation techniques and agendas to keep team members and stakeholders engaged in every sprint review.

Skipping It

When a Scrum team doesn't achieve their sprint goal, some teams choose to cancel the sprint review to avoid embarrassment or punishment. Canceling a sprint review to avoid bad feelings is a sign that there's a lack of trust in an organization. Delaying bad news only makes the news worse when it's finally reported. It may sound counterintuitive, but holding a sprint review

---

1. http://liberatingstructures.com

Joe asks:
Who takes notes during a sprint review?

We often see Scrum teams leaving a sprint review without any notes about what happened during the event. The product owner is accountable for updating and adapting the product backlog, but that's not to say that the product owner is the only person who should take notes. In fact, *everyone* should take notes in a sprint review. Some of the best Scrum teams we've worked with sit and compare notes soon after the sprint review. This may occur ad hoc, in sprint planning, or right after the review, before the retrospective. After gathering everyone's perspective, the product owner can then adapt the product backlog accordingly.

is *exactly* what the Scrum teams needs to do when problems occur because it will help them build trust in the organization.

Scrum teams skip sprint reviews for many reasons:

- They failed to achieve the sprint goal.

- They need just a little more time to accomplish the sprint goal and will hold the event after the next sprint.

- Only one or two stakeholders are available to attend.

- Some team members are out of the office.

- The organization has a "clean the plate" mentality (see Chapter 10, Sprint Planning, on page 119 for more on this anti-pattern), and the team didn't complete the entire sprint backlog.

- There was an impediment that slowed the team down and they have nothing to present.

Regardless of the reason for canceling, it's important to keep in mind that there's no such thing as a failed sprint. Every sprint is an opportunity to learn something about the product, your organization, and the complexity of the work that you're doing. As we discussed earlier in this chapter, the sprint review is much more than a demo. Alongside stakeholders, the Scrum team should evaluate changes in market conditions, the state of the product backlog, and any problems that they've encountered.

Skipping the sprint review reduces the transparency of the product-development effort. You lose an opportunity to inspect the increment with stakeholders, regardless of its completeness. Forgoing this inspection point adds risk to the project. The Scrum team can't adapt their approach in an informed way because they haven't sought out the opinions of outsiders—the stakeholders.

I said "Skip It"
by: Todd Miller

Some of the stories we've shared in this book were hard to write about. This is the hardest one for me.

I was the Scrum master on a project and we were in crunch mode. We were optimistic throughout the sprint that the increment was looking good and the sprint goal was achievable. But then, two days away from the sprint review, we ran into technical problems with a third-party library we depended on. The day before the review, I strongly recommended to the team that we cancel the sprint review because we weren't going to have anything to show. So we canceled it.

Our stakeholders didn't say anything and didn't seem bothered by the cancellation. We planned our next sprint with the same sprint goal and pushed forward. We solved the problems during that sprint, but it ended up requiring a Herculean effort.

During the next sprint review—the first one we'd held in many weeks—the Scrum team talked about the problems we had faced, showed working software, and discussed where we were heading. About halfway through the review, a stakeholder commented that the solution we were building was not that important and that we should have spent our time doing something else. Anger erupted in the room, and the product owner bore the brunt of it. It was tense and really struck us hard. We learned the hard way that canceling even one sprint review could result in the team heading in the wrong direction, because we didn't have timely input from stakeholders. We agreed to never cancel a sprint review again.

Don't cancel the sprint review, no matter how much easier you think it may make things for the Scrum team. Hold the event no matter how hard it is to do so. As a Scrum masters, it's up to you to make sure this event happens. If you and your team end up in a situation where you're worried the sprint review will be uncomfortable, try adding the following to your agenda:

- These activities happened during the sprint:…
- These impediments got in our way:…
- The complexities we are facing are…
- Currently our product backlog contains…
- Does what happened change the future of the product?

Facing the music in an uncomfortable sprint review now is far better than skipping it and taking the risk that the team may head in the wrong direction, resulting in an even worse sprint review in the future. Live the Scrum value of courage and hold every sprint review so you can work with stakeholders to conquer whatever problems your team encounters.

The Standing Ovation

Todd was a Scrum master for a team whose organization had never done Scrum before. At the end of the sprint review, stakeholders were so impressed at seeing working software after a mere two weeks of work that they stood up, clapping and cheering for the Scrum team. The team walked out of the event with their heads held high, feeling euphoric. During the sprint retrospective, the Scrum team was still riding high off the impression they had on the stakeholders. Team members couldn't think of many improvements to suggest because of their heightened sense of optimism. They decided that they should just keep doing what they did the last sprint.

Two sprint reviews later, the euphoria wore off quickly, as stakeholders from the accounting department asked tough questions and appeared very disappointed at the results of the increment. They questioned the decisions the team was making and demanded answers on the allocation of budget for such meager results. During the retrospective, the Scrum team was devastated. They were in shock from what had just happened and were desperate to find ways to go back to the days of applause and cheering. Just a few short weeks ago they had been heroes, but at that moment they felt like failures.

It's important that the Scrum team set clear expectations with stakeholders as to why the stakeholders attend sprint reviews. It's not an event designed to punish or reward the Scrum team. Rather, it's an opportunity for the stakeholders to inspect what's happened, provide feedback, and decide what to do next. If the stakeholders do reward or punish the Scrum team during a sprint review, it's important for you, the Scrum master, to immediately remind the stakeholders why they're involved in the sprint review, and to refocus their attention on the increment and what the team should do next.

This kind of scenario is a classic carrot-and-stick model: We'll clap if you do something we like and we'll yell if you do something we don't. The result is a reward and punishment system that makes people fixate on chasing the reward. But if the team focuses on getting the reward, that will prevent tough conversations that need to happen in a sprint review between the Scrum team and stakeholders, for the good of the project.

A super useful book that can help you deal with this anti-pattern is *Drive* by Daniel Pink.[2] It contains some excellent info about what motivates human beings. You can use the lessons you learn from it in your organization. We consider *Drive* a must-read for all Scrum masters.

---

2.   https://www.danpink.com/drive./

Coach's Corner

The sprint review is a collaborative event for the Scrum team and stakeholders. It's an opportunity to huddle with people outside the team to evaluate the state of the increment. As Scrum masters, we must constantly find new ways to create transparency around what's happening so that we give the Scrum team an opportunity to make informed decisions about what should happen next.

In order to ensure that your sprint reviews are as valuable as possible, prior to your next sprint review, ask yourself these questions:

- Are the right people involved in sprint reviews so that the product backlog can be adapted in an informed way?

- Is it clear why we did what we did this sprint?

- Does everyone attending the sprint review know why the Scrum team is building this product?

- Are we going to give stakeholders any misconceptions about where we truly are?

- Is the entire Scrum team in alignment about what has happened during the sprint?

- Are we recycling the same agenda as last time?

The answers to these questions may help you spot areas where your sprint review is lacking. It might be worthwhile posing these questions to the rest of the Scrum team to gain their perspectives, too.

In the next chapter, we turn our attention to the sprint retrospective, an event that focuses on continuous improvement. The retrospective is vitally important to the success of any Scrum team.

CHAPTER 15

The Sprint Retrospective

Todd worked with a Scrum team that was adding new features to a fitness application. They had just completed their second sprint review, with many stakeholders present. There were a few tense moments between the stakeholders and the product owner but overall the sprint review was a success.

Immediately afterward, the development team and Scrum master gathered for the sprint retrospective. Here's how it unfolded:

> *Matt [developer]:* *I'd really like to try some pair programming next sprint. I'm struggling a bit to understand the one pattern that we're using. I mean, I'm doing it, but I'm just not sure it's the best way. It would be nice to have an extra set of eyes.*

> *Peter [developer]:* *I disagree. We're getting a ton done working the way we are now. You saw it—the stakeholders and product owner are happy, so why mess with our approach? Matt, I'll send you an online article about the pattern. You should be understanding this by now. I don't understand why you're not picking it up.*

> *Other developers:* *[Silent, awkwardly staring down at notepads.]*

> *Scrum Master:* *This seems like an opportunity, perhaps a chance to try some pair programming. Who wants to try that with Matt?*

> *Peter:* *I'm out. I don't have time for that—it's a complete waste of time. My improvement for this next sprint is for us to get better at estimating. I've got to go. It's time for lunch, and my time is better spent coding than sitting in meetings. You're the Scrum master—you keep the product owner and stakeholders happy while we code. Your job is to keep us out of meetings. My job is to actually deliver things. [Storms out.]*

Every sprint after that, the tension kept rising until development team members rarely spoke. The product they delivered to the customer reflected the lack of communication within the team—the application was buggy and the user interface wasn't cohesive. After several conversations and chances, the customer fired the entire team because of their inability to get the job done.

Each sprint retrospective is a chance for the Scrum team to reaffirm its commitment to continuous improvement. A team uses the time to reflect on team dynamics, quality, defining "done," and seeking ways to improve the way we deliver potentially releasable products every sprint. Without approaching this event openly and finding ways to improve every sprint, your product, its quality, and the people working together on it will suffer.

Scrum is just a framework. People are the power behind the roles, events, and artifacts. If we as a team are not collaborating, helping, supporting, and challenging ourselves to improve, we're missing a crucial opportunity to improve the way we serve our customers.

In this chapter, we explore some of the sprint retrospective anti-patterns that Scrum teams experience. Remember that there are two sides to Scrum: the people and the technology—and during a retrospective, the team needs to explore both.

Few Bother to Attend

Some Scrum teams take an unenthusiastic approach to the sprint retrospective. For example, the product owner we mentioned at the beginning of this chapter attended the sprint review but not the sprint retrospective. That was a big missed opportunity, as the retrospective would have been the opportune time for the PO to talk to the development team about how to mitigate future stakeholder surprises. Similar problems may pop up if development team members don't attend the retrospective.

The sprint retrospective is an activity for the *whole* Scrum team. It should include all development team members, the product owner, and the Scrum master—every time. The only way the team can improve is if the whole team engages in this event. Dysfunction cannot be fixed when there is only partial attendance.

Also, keep in mind that this event is for the Scrum team *only*. When stakeholders or managers outside the team attend, that makes it harder for the team to effectively collaborate. It's hard enough to get a group of people from different backgrounds, cultures, and experiences to collaborate. Adding another layer of difficulty doesn't help.

Consider the reason behind the sprint retrospective: You're meeting to inspect the way the Scrum team works together, as team members strive to deliver a done increment of product by the end of the sprint. The adaptations (a.k.a. improvements) that the team agrees upon and commits to during the retrospective can help the team deliver value to customers more quickly.

You should also use the sprint retrospective to consider quality. Discuss the current definition of done and decide whether it needs to be modified based on what you learned about your product during the sprint review.

If the entire team isn't present for these discussions, you could lose transparency in the way you're working; any experiments that you try might not get the intended results. So get your entire Scrum team to attend the retrospective.

> **Joe asks:**
> ## When should the sprint retrospective happen?
>
> It should always happen after the sprint review but before the next sprint planning. That's because, if you haven't inspected the increment and how you're collaborating with stakeholders, then you haven't fully inspected the sprint. This can lead to adaptations that aren't appropriate for your situation.
>
> As far as duration, The Scrum Guide states that a sprint retrospective time box is a maximum of three hours for a one-month sprint. Adjust that time box accordingly based on your sprint length.

Superficial Commitments

Let's say a team has a decent sprint, and after inspecting the increment during the sprint review, the team members gather for the retrospective. They collaborate on a list of ideas that could help them improve the way they work. Then they select two items that they think will help them improve during the next sprint:

1. Update the definition of done to include code reviews before checking code into source control.

2. Restrict coffee talk to outside the team room because it's distracting to some team members.

The next sprint starts, but the team completely ignores the two improvements they committed to. Despite the Scrum master reminding them about it, they've become lost in the work and are too busy to implement the code review change. And coffee chatter happens frequently in the team room—in fact, it's more noticeable than ever.

This pattern continues for several sprints. Eventually code quality goes down and the production bug rate spikes. The team is also experiencing a rise in conflicts. They aren't improving. In fact, in some ways, they're moving backward.

It's important that the Scrum team live by the Scrum values in everything they do. Team members must truly commit to the improvements that the team identifies in the retrospective. Team members must commit to one another on making the improvements. Ignoring these commitments is a clear sign that the team hasn't embraced a mindset of continuous improvement.

If your team has fallen into this trap of creating superficial commitments but not following through with them, you can use a few techniques to try to fix that. During the next retrospective, begin by asking members how the team did with their previous improvement items. Remember, these improvement experiments are sprint backlog items, so the team should consider them each day during the daily scrum and perhaps even discuss them during the sprint review.

If the team didn't make progress, then you need to talk about why. Did the team forget to account for the time it would take to complete the improvement item during sprint planning? Perhaps it was unclear how the team would make or measure the progress of the experiment? In any case, the team needs to have an open and respectful discussion to help team members commit to improving during their next sprint.

 Joe asks:
How many improvements are reasonable?

An ambitious team might identify many improvements they wish to work on in the next sprint, but committing to an excessive amount might mean that none actually get accomplished. Keep in mind that improvements impact the team's capacity during the sprint. Taking on more than one or two improvement items may not lead to the business outcomes that the product owner and stakeholders are expecting. Scrum teams should select just a few key improvements that they believe they can implement during the next sprint. Work as a team to determine the right number of improvements for each sprint.

Meaningless Improvements

Let's suppose the Scrum master facilitates an interactive session with the whole team in attendance, and team members respond with some ideas for how they can get better. Here's what they came up with:

- Have more fun
- Go to lunch once a week
- Write better code
- Estimate with more accuracy
- Collaborate

Are these actionable improvements? Will this team really get better if they choose to implement one or two of these items in the next sprint? The items are awfully vague and they don't make for concrete improvements. It's great that the entire Scrum team attended the sprint retrospective and that team members are generating ideas about how to improve—but now it's time to delve into the team's problems to find root causes and measurable goals and objectives for the next sprint.

The retrospective is about examining people, relationships, and technical practices that are inhibiting the team. Let's review the items that the team came up with, and add some follow-up questions you might ask to dig a little deeper into the problems:

- Have more fun
  - Is someone killing all the fun?
  - What's preventing this team from thinking work is fun?
  - When's the last time the team was shown appreciation during a sprint retrospective?
- Go to lunch once a week
  - Is everybody getting along?
  - What are we going to solve by going to lunch?
  - Are we not communicating well enough?
- Write better code
  - What's our definition of quality?
  - Are we writing bad code?
  - Is the architecture still appropriate given what we know now?
  - Should we revisit our definition of done?
- Estimate with more accuracy
  - Why are we estimating?
  - What did we estimate incorrectly?
  - Did our bad estimate set unrealistic expectations?
  - Are there impediments or bad practices that impact our ability to estimate?
- Collaborate
  - Are we helping each other?
  - What happened between the development team and product owner?
  - Are we missing opportunities to work together?
  - Are we appropriately refining the product backlog?

Empty improvements are the easy way to get out of a retrospective quickly, but they invoke no real improvements. The team has to dig deep into relationships and/or technical issues in order to reach its maximum potential. The retrospective should be as serious and professional a meeting as the sprint review. It's the time to bring up issues and attempt to find resolutions.

As a Scrum master, you'll need to flex your facilitation muscles and discover what questions lead to the right conversations to help reveal the deeper issues. Keep digging—your teams need you.

50% Participation

Talking and sharing opinions may come easily to some people, but it can be a real struggle for others who are from a different culture or have a different background or personality type. Some participants might be very uncomfortable when the topic of discussion is something as sensitive as "what can we do to get better?" The meeting can then become dominated by only a few people, leaving silent the ideas and opinions of the rest of the room. If there's a strong voice or personality in the room that creates conflict, attendees may further shut down.

There are many methods you can use to facilitate a retrospective. The best ones will help you draw out problems and ideas from *everybody* in the room. You have to find creative ways to gauge the team's safety level—how comfortable team members feel about sharing candid opinions and receiving critical feedback.

You may, at times, feel like you have a good read on the room. We have sometimes felt confident that we had a room of people figured out, only to find that we were wrong. There's no substitute for getting direct feedback from the team. For example, you can gauge team safety anonymously by issuing a survey and then sharing the results. What's important is that everyone feels safe and that everyone has an equal voice. Be sure to experiment with different methods to ensure that every team member is heard.

For example, here's a simple technique that you can try during your next sprint retrospective. It's called The Starfish Retrospective, and it's a great way to find out what a Scrum team can change about the way they work during a sprint. Here's what you do:

1. Draw a star on a whiteboard or flip chart and label the five sections: Start,"Stop," More,"Less," and "Keep" Explain to your team that the various sections should contain answers to these questions:

   • Start: What does the team want to start doing during the next sprint to improve the way they work together and deliver products?

- Stop: What are the things that don't bring value to the team and should be stopped before the next sprint?

- More: What are the things we're doing well that we need more of on our team?

- Less: Which activities burn more time and energy than the value they create?

- Keep: What are the practices, experiments, or ideas that we need to keep because we've seen them generate positive changes that we want to preserve?

2. Ask the participants to generate as many ideas for each area as possible. Give a few minutes for each participant to place their comments on the board and read them out loud.

3. When all the areas have been filled, facilitate a short discussion about what the team shared. Point out trends and patterns.

4. Ask each person to vote for one Start item and one Stop item that resonates with them the most.

5. Explore the Start and Stop items that got the most votes, then generate measurable changes or experiments to try during the next sprint.

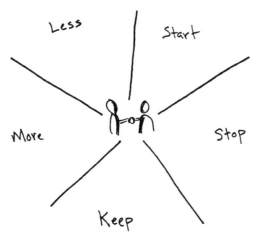

For more ideas and sprint retrospective formats to experiment with, visit TastyCupcakes.[1] There you'll find an extensive collection of formats and ideas that you can use to help your Scrum teams explore ways to improve how they work.

---

1. http://tastycupcakes.org/tag/retrospective/

Joe asks:

Where should sprint retrospective results be displayed?

There isn't a clear consensus on this. Some teams add improvements to the product backlog as a product backlog item because those improvements add value to the increment. Other teams display them in the team room where they hold their daily scrum. Whatever your team decides, make sure your improvements are displayed in a place where the team gets reminded of them and can take action on them.

Be cautious about storing retrospective results in a public tool where management can see them. Depending on the level of trust in your organization, this can decrease your team's willingness to be open and honest about problems they're experiencing. On the flip side, sharing these results publicly could help other teams that are struggling with similar issues.

Skipping It

When faced with outside pressures or critical deadlines, some Scrum teams will cancel the sprint retrospective. Cancelling a retrospective because a team needs the time to work is a symptom of dysfunction. In these situations, a retrospective is *exactly* what a team needs.

When working in a complex domain where outcomes are more unknown than known, a Scrum team needs to take time to think about how members are working together, and adapt their approach as needed. Outside pressure is a sign that there might be organizational dysfunction that the team isn't dealing with appropriately. It's important to inspect where outside pressures are coming from, and create a plan for resolving those issues. A lack of transparency to the world outside the Scrum team is often the culprit.

How can you convince your team to hold the retrospective, even when they feel there's no time for it? Here are some questions you can ask the team when they're trying to skip the retrospective:

- Where are the pressures we're feeling coming from?
- The time we get back by canceling—is that going to be the difference between success and failure?
- How did the deadline we're facing come to be?
- Is our architecture stable and appropriate for the product?
- Is technical debt readily apparent in what we're building?

Sometimes You Have to Sneak In a Retrospective

by: Ryan Ripley

During an especially busy sprint, the Scrum team insisted on skipping the sprint retrospective so they could keep working. Instead of arguing with the team, I decided to ask a simple question: "What happened during the sprint that created this pressure at the end of the sprint?" A developer quickly replied that the product backlog items were unclear, and that the development team ran into a few surprises along the way. So I asked, "Is there anything we could do during the next sprint to help avoid this situation?" Another developer suggested holding refinement sessions to work on PBIs prior to sprint planning. I smiled and encouraged them to add this idea to their sprint backlog for the next sprint.

You see what I did there? Simply by asking a couple of questions, I managed to hold a mini, impromptu sprint retrospective.

Here are the things that I learned from this situation:

- This exchange took five minutes and the team had improvements for the next sprint.
- Sometimes we have to be clever in the way we work with immature Scrum teams.
- Keep the purpose of the sprint retrospective in mind. In this brief interaction, we got a good improvement idea quickly. Claim the win and move on.

A retrospective should never be canceled because there isn't enough time for it. It's the Scrum team's opportunity to inspect *why* they don't have time and adapt so they don't feel that way again. Canceling the retrospective is putting a bandage on a wound that's only going to get worse over time. Per The Scrum Guide, the time box for a retrospective is three hours for a four-week sprint, so what time are you really getting back? If three hours can make or break your four-week sprint, you need to reveal the deeper issues.

The Complaint Session

Scrum teams often live in an agile bubble within their organizations. To team members, the outside world can seem strange, ridiculous, or even behind the times. Influences from elsewhere in the organization can impact a Scrum team, creating an "us vs. them" mentality. For these and other reasons, sprint retrospectives can spiral into complaint sessions.

For example, it's common for Scrum teams to complain about management and how they "don't get it." This isn't an empathetic view of people in your organization. Instead of letting the team vent about management during a retrospective, ask them how they may have contributed to the manager's behavior. This forces them to take personal responsibility and own the problem.

Why isn't our manager leaving us alone?

by: Todd Miller

I was the Scrum master of a team whose organization had just begun adopting Scrum. Several sprints in, during a retrospective, the team began to vent about someone who was always trying to add work to their sprint backlog and insert himself into every Scrum event. It was becoming very disruptive. I joined in the complaining, not understanding why this manager was so adamant that he be included in everything.

On my drive home from work that day, I felt guilty for joining the complaining. To redeem myself, I decided the best course of action was to display the Scrum value of courage and sit down with the manager to see what he was feeling. As it turned out, he was only a few years from retirement and was concerned about what his place in the organization was going to be moving forward. In his eyes, it seemed that the team was doing great and that he wasn't needed anymore.

I worked with this manager and the team quite a bit to create empathy and understanding on both sides. Continuing to complain without action would have raised the tension and stunted the organization's ability to successfully adopt Scrum. To this day, I wish I'd have facilitated during that retrospective instead of complained.

As a Scrum master, you should consider both complaining and blaming to be red flags. You need to be aware of the dangers of complaining. It builds a culture of negativity and helplessness where problems aren't solved, but are only discussed. Steer the conversation back to how the Scrum team can own the impediment or issue they're discussing. This is much more productive in the long run and helps your team practice crucial skills like self-organization and complex problem-solving. Help your teams *own* their issues and find ways to creatively solve their problems.

Complaining gets a team no closer to a resolution. If you see the conversation spiraling into a complaint session, steer your team back to problem-solving.

Coach's Corner

You need to ensure that retrospectives don't become repetitive, as that can cause stagnation among the team. Regularly experiment with new retrospective formats that can draw the best ideas from everyone in the room. Each retrospective is an opportunity for you to be creative and explore new techniques.

Sometimes you can solve problems simply by getting all the team members to attend the sprint retrospective and come up with a few (but not *too* many) actionable improvements. Then the team must live the Scrum values of commitment and focus to uphold and implement those improvements.

Ask the teams these questions regularly:

- Is our quality getting better?
- Do we feel like a team?

- Are we living the Scrum values?
- Has our definition of done become more strict?
- What's slowing us down, both technically and organizationally?
- How is the product owner/development team relationship?
- How are our relationships with people outside the Scrum team?
- Are we proud of the work we're doing?

When used correctly, sprint retrospectives are a great tool to help keep your team moving forward in a positive way. It's vital that they happen and are fruitful in outcomes that create solid improvements for the team. You, as a Scrum master, are accountable for making sure that happens.

Index

Thank you!

How did you enjoy this book? Please let us know. Take a moment and email us at support@pragprog.com with your feedback. Tell us your story and you could win free ebooks. Please use the subject line "Book Feedback."

Ready for your next great Pragmatic Bookshelf book? Come on over to https://pragprog.com and use the coupon code BUYANOTHER2020 to save 30% on your next ebook.

Void where prohibited, restricted, or otherwise unwelcome. Do not use ebooks near water. If rash persists, see a doctor. Doesn't apply to *The Pragmatic Programmer* ebook because it's older than the Pragmatic Bookshelf itself. Side effects may include increased knowledge and skill, increased marketability, and deep satisfaction. Increase dosage regularly.

And thank you for your continued support,

Andy Hunt, Publisher

Software Estimation Without Guessing

Developers hate estimation, and most managers fear disappointment with the results, but there is hope for both. You'll have to give up some widely held misconceptions: let go of the notion that "an estimate is an estimate," and estimate for your particular need. Realize that estimates have a limited shelf-life, and re-estimate frequently as needed. When reality differs from your estimate, don't lament; mine that disappointment for the gold that can be the longer-term jackpot. We'll show you how.

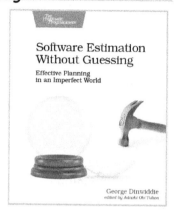

George Dinwiddie
(246 pages) ISBN: 9781680506983. $29.95
https://pragprog.com/book/gdestimate

Designing Elixir Systems with OTP

You know how to code in Elixir; now learn to think in it. Learn to design libraries with intelligent layers that shape the right data structures, flow from one function into the next, and present the right APIs. Embrace the same OTP that's kept our telephone systems reliable and fast for over 30 years. Move beyond understanding the OTP functions to knowing what's happening under the hood, and why that matters. Using that knowledge, instinctively know how to design systems that deliver fast and resilient services to your users, all with an Elixir focus.

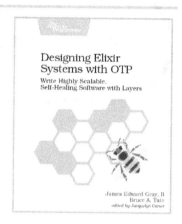

James Edward Gray, II and Bruce A. Tate
(246 pages) ISBN: 9781680506617. $41.95
https://pragprog.com/book/jgotp

Programming Phoenix 1.4

Don't accept the compromise between fast and beautiful: you can have it all. Phoenix creator Chris McCord, Elixir creator José Valim, and award-winning author Bruce Tate walk you through building an application that's fast and reliable. At every step, you'll learn from the Phoenix creators not just what to do, but why. Packed with insider insights and completely updated for Phoenix 1.4, this definitive guide will be your constant companion in your journey from Phoenix novice to expert as you build the next generation of web applications.

Chris McCord, Bruce Tate and José Valim
(356 pages) ISBN: 9781680502268. $45.95
https://pragprog.com/book/phoenix14

Programming Kotlin

Programmers don't just use Kotlin, they love it. Even Google has adopted it as a first-class language for Android development. With Kotlin, you can intermix imperative, functional, and object-oriented styles of programming and benefit from the approach that's most suitable for the problem at hand. Learn to use the many features of this highly concise, fluent, elegant, and expressive statically typed language with easy-to-understand examples. Learn to write maintainable, high-performing JVM and Android applications, create DSLs, program asynchronously, and much more.

Venkat Subramaniam
(460 pages) ISBN: 9781680506358. $51.95
https://pragprog.com/book/vskotlin

Programming Elm

Elm brings the safety and stability of functional pro-
graming to front-end development, making it one of
the most popular new languages. Elm's functional nature and static typing means that runtime errors are
nearly impossible, and it compiles to JavaScript for
easy web deployment. This book helps you take advantage of this new language in your web site development.
Learn how the Elm Architecture will help you create
fast applications. Discover how to integrate Elm with
JavaScript so you can update legacy applications. See
how Elm tooling makes deployment quicker and easier.

Jeremy Fairbank
(308 pages) ISBN: 9781680502855. $40.95
https://pragprog.com/book/jfelm

Technical Blogging, Second Edition

Successful technical blogging is not easy but it's also
not magic. Use these techniques to attract and keep
an audience of loyal, regular readers. Leverage this
popularity to reach your goals and amplify your influence in your field. Get more users for your startup or
open source project, or simply find an outlet to share
your expertise. This book is your blueprint, with step-
by-step instructions that leave no stone unturned.
Plan, create, maintain, and promote a successful blog
that will have remarkable effects on your career or
business.

Antonio Cangiano
(336 pages) ISBN: 9781680506471. $47.95
https://pragprog.com/book/actb2

Build Chatbot Interactions

The next step in the evolution of user interfaces is here. Chatbots let your users interact with your service in their own natural language. Use free and open source tools along with Ruby to build creative, useful, and unexpected interactions for users. Take advantage of the Lita framework's step-by-step implementation strategy to simplify bot development and testing. From novices to experts, chatbots are an area in which everyone can participate. Exercise your creativity by creating chatbot skills for communicating, information, and fun.

Daniel Pritchett
(206 pages) ISBN: 9781680506327. $35.95
https://pragprog.com/book/dpchat

Test-Driven React

You work in a loop: write code, get feedback, iterate. The faster you get feedback, the faster you can learn and become a more effective developer. Test-Driven React helps you refine your React workflow to give you the feedback you need as quickly as possible. Write strong tests and run them continuously as you work, split complex code up into manageable pieces, and stay focused on what's important by automating away mundane, trivial tasks. Adopt these techniques and you'll be able to avoid productivity traps and start building React components at a stunning pace!

Trevor Burnham
(190 pages) ISBN: 9781680506464. $45.95
https://pragprog.com/book/tbreact

Small, Sharp Software Tools

The command-line interface is making a comeback. That's because developers know that all the best features of your operating system are hidden behind a user interface designed to help average people use the computer. But you're not the average user, and the CLI is the most efficient way to get work done fast. Turn tedious chores into quick tasks: read and write files, manage complex directory hierarchies, perform network diagnostics, download files, work with APIs, and combine individual programs to create your own workflows. Put down that mouse, open the CLI, and take control of your software development environment.

Brian P. Hogan
(326 pages) ISBN: 9781680502961. $38.95
https://pragprog.com/book/bhcldev

Programming Ecto

Languages may come and go, but the relational database endures. Learn how to use Ecto, the premier database library for Elixir, to connect your Elixir and Phoenix apps to databases. Get a firm handle on Ecto fundamentals with a module-by-module tour of the critical parts of Ecto. Then move on to more advanced topics and advice on best practices with a series of recipes that provide clear, step-by-step instructions on scenarios commonly encountered by app developers. Co-authored by the creator of Ecto, this title provides all the essentials you need to use Ecto effectively.

Darin Wilson and Eric Meadows-Jönsson
(242 pages) ISBN: 9781680502824. $45.95
https://pragprog.com/book/wmecto

Web Development with ReasonML

ReasonML is a new, type-safe, functional language that compiles to efficient, readable JavaScript. ReasonML interoperates with existing JavaScript libraries and works especially well with React, one of the most popular front-end frameworks. Learn how to take advantage of the power of a functional language while keeping the flexibility of the whole JavaScript ecosystem. Move beyond theory and get things done faster and more reliably with ReasonML today.

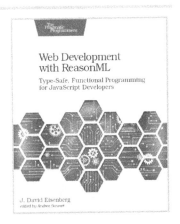

J. David Eisenberg
(208 pages) ISBN: 9781680506334. $45.95
https://pragprog.com/book/reasonml

Programming WebAssembly with Rust

WebAssembly fulfills the long-awaited promise of web technologies: fast code, type-safe at compile time, execution in the browser, on embedded devices, or anywhere else. Rust delivers the power of C in a language that strictly enforces type safety. Combine both languages and you can write for the web like never before! Learn how to integrate with JavaScript, run code on platforms other than the browser, and take a step into IoT. Discover the easy way to build cross-platform applications without sacrificing power, and change the way you write code for the web.

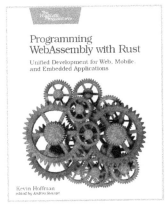

Kevin Hoffman
(238 pages) ISBN: 9781680506365. $45.95
https://pragprog.com/book/khrust

The Pragmatic Bookshelf

The Pragmatic Bookshelf features books written by professional developers for professional developers. The titles continue the well-known Pragmatic Programmer style and continue to garner awards and rave reviews. As development gets more and more difficult, the Pragmatic Programmers will be there with more titles and products to help you stay on top of your game.

Visit Us Online

This Book's Home Page
https://pragprog.com/book/rrscrum
Source code from this book, errata, and other resources. Come give us feedback, too!

Keep Up to Date
https://pragprog.com
Join our announcement mailing list (low volume) or follow us on twitter @pragprog for new titles, sales, coupons, hot tips, and more.

New and Noteworthy
https://pragprog.com/news
Check out the latest pragmatic developments, new titles and other offerings.

Save on the ebook

Save on the ebook versions of this title. Owning the paper version of this book entitles you to purchase the electronic versions at a terrific discount.

PDFs are great for carrying around on your laptop—they are hyperlinked, have color, and are fully searchable. Most titles are also available for the iPhone and iPod touch, Amazon Kindle, and other popular e-book readers.

Buy now at *https://pragprog.com/coupon*

Contact Us

Online Orders:	*https://pragprog.com/catalog*
Customer Service:	*support@pragprog.com*
International Rights:	*translations@pragprog.com*
Academic Use:	*academic@pragprog.com*
Write for Us:	*http://write-for-us.pragprog.com*
Or Call:	+1 800-699-7764